Bread an

*Lessons learnt building a successful
company from scratch*

The best possible advice comes from someone who has actually done it. Tim provides an honest and humble account of his creation of this amazing business. If you have any ambition to ever run something yourself, this book will provide you with some great straightforward guidance.

Charles Dunstone – Founder & Chief Executive, Carphone Warehouse

This is a fantastic book from someone who really has been there, done that and made a fortune from nothing but a good business idea. Packed with brilliantly useful advice and guidance, this book is a must-read for any budding entrepreneur.

**Rachel Bridge – Enterprise Editor of the *Sunday Times*
and author of four books about entrepreneurs**

I strongly recommend this inspiring book of a real business on a roller-coaster to success. It provides a chance to look inside the head of a successful entrepreneur and contains invaluable advice to anyone wanting to run their own business.   **Geoff Quinn – Chief Executive, T M Lewin**

This narrative of the birth and sale of what became a successful business turns out to be a remarkable and practical evocation of leadership. Roupell's grace and persistence enable him to land the bread 'butter-side up'.

Marcus Gregson – Founder Chief Executive of HSBC Private Bank

Much has been written about the importance of the big idea but we have eaten bread for thousands of years and businesses still make good money out of selling it. You don't have to be novel to make money, you just have to do it a bit better than the next person. You are more likely to make a profit doing something which has been tried and tested. Tim's story is the best example of this, and an inspiration to any aspiring entrepreneur.

Nick Jenkins – Founder of moonpig.com

A stimulating and exciting read of a business cycle from start to success, with highs and lows, but above all containing a rich seam of practical advice and ideas that is as relevant to a newly-formed business as it is to a large corporation.   **Rory Tapner – Chief Executive of Coutts**

Bread and Butter

Lessons learnt building a
successful company from scratch

TIM ROUPELL

To Josh
Good luck!
Tim

QUARTET BOOKS

First published in 2011 by
Quartet Books Limited
A member of the Namara Group
27 Goodge Street, London WIT 2LD

A catalogue record for this book
is available from the British Library

ISBN 978 0 7043 7243 6

Typeset by Antony Gray
Printed and bound in Great Britain by
T J International Ltd, Padstow, Cornwall

This book is dedicated to Seham Ahmedein, the heart and soul of Daily Bread – our Mother Hen and Sergeant Major – and to whom I am forever indebted.

Contents

Size Matters – Kiss (keep it simple, stupid) – Don't
be Average – Cash Counts – Watch the Bottom
Line – Keep Positive – Language is Important –
Listen – Learn from Mistakes – Grasp the Nettle –
Don't Lie – Appreciation – Be in the Room –
Choose your Response – Learn to Breathe – Save
your Breath – Keep on Moving – Write down your
Goals – Hiring and Firing – Letting Go – Culture is
Critical – Stand up to Bullies – Silence is Golden –
Learn to Switch Off – Earn or Learn – Use Experts –
Trust your Instincts – To Avoid Seasickness, Look
to the Horizon – Good Luck

Acknowledgements

My wife Harriet and our children. No man could ask for more . . .

With sincere thanks to the following, all of whom have been sources of help or inspiration:

David Mathewson, Graham Harrison, Marcus Gregson, Abel Hadden, Andrew Scott, Simon Denehy, Simon Robertson-Macleod, Julian Grazebrook, Hugh & Moux Lowther, Kate Slessor, Peter McPhillips, James Knight-Adams, Terry Ryder, Gill Levett, Rowan Southerland, Sarah Whitefield, David Singh, Tom Price, Harvey Rose, Michael Todd, Lyndsey Allen, Wendy Fry, Murray Tollemache, Poonam, Ellie, Cassandra, Sergio, Ebeneezar, Ram, Kamel, and everyone that ever worked at Daily Bread.

Also to Edward Griffiths, Mark Flanagan, Noel Mahoney, Terry Cook, Paul Ettinger, Chris Copner, David Stearne, Oliver Leatham and all our clients and suppliers for your loyalty and support over the years.

And special thanks also to all those bastards – the landlords and young punks in purchasing departments – who inadvertently helped motivate, inspire and push me further than I would ever have gone by myself!

Finally, to Rachel Bridge who rashly insisted I write this book and without whose encouragement it would never have happened.

Introduction

If I had known then what I know now, would I have ever started? I have been asked this question quite often over the years and the answer has never been straightforward. My instinctive reply would often be, 'You must be joking . . . ' The reason for this is that it has been a roller coaster of a ride during which I was often pushed to my physical and mental limits. Before I started I thought that it would be easy, in fact it must be easy – who can't make a sandwich? And what would I do with myself in the afternoons after the lunchtime rush? Zero games of golf, a huge amount of work, and ten years later I'd done not much more than survive off the business and was in the process of going bust. On the other hand, I read a quote a few years ago along the lines of success being all the sweeter for the struggle, and that resonates as well. I have ended up being extremely fortunate and so the answer can now only be a resounding, 'Yes.' It just didn't always feel that way . . .

Prologue

The point of writing this book is to try and show that building up a profitable business turning over many millions of pounds from scratch and with no money or experience is possible for anyone. It's by no means always easy, and that will become clear as I go along, and you do need a good dollop of luck. But it *is* possible and as the saying goes, if I can do it, anyone can. This is not false modesty, simply a matter of fact. I am not clever, and can't remember a thing unless I'm interested in it. I'm pretty lazy by nature and while fear may have been my main driver, the other one was the beach. If I could make enough money then I could retire and sit on a beach all day – now there was a target worth heading for! The fact that I would now get bored rigid after a day or two of this is beside the point – it acted as a great spur and inspiration. You need a target to aim for to help raise your head occasionally, and my target would be the beach. I would be driven by the beach.

So what did I know about business when I set up Daily Bread? Absolutely nothing. I just knew that I couldn't keep complaining about working for other people and the time had come to work for myself.

Apart from my direct experiences, I have also read some books that had a major influence on me, and for six years I spent one day each month with ten fellow entrepreneurs (through an organisation called the Academy of Chief Executives) discussing our business problems in detail. This made me realise that we all had similar issues (usually centred around people) and that most businesses have very similar issues, regardless of their size or sector. Some great things came out of these meetings, lessons that I use to this day, and they have helped provide some of the motivation to write this book.

All's well that ends well; however, there were moments of intense self-doubt and lack of confidence, when the struggle seemed futile and physical and mental energies were at rock bottom. Times when, as Winston Churchill put it, you had to just keep buggering on. I wanted to put down what I have learnt while I have been buggering on, in the hope that it may be of some value to someone, somewhere, sometime.

The best way I could think of doing this was to tell the chronological story of Daily Bread, from its embryonic start to eventual sale and, to begin with, a little background as to where my drive and motivation came from. The Daily Bread story starts on page 27.

Life before Daily Bread: Childhood

I believe the two main drivers in business are fear and greed. I have always been primarily driven by fear, and, as I grew older, an increasing determination to control my own destiny. To be my own man.

It is difficult to pinpoint where the fear came from. I was brought up in a very loving family with three brothers and one sister. My father was in the army and so we were abroad for most of my childhood in Germany, Aden and Hong Kong, moving every two years. Not good for making long-term childhood friends, but great for meeting new people and, being such a large family, we were very self-contained and have always had a lot of fun together. I am number three and my two elder brothers, Anthony and David, could not be more different. Anthony was very athletic and good looking with straight black hair and found life generally easy. He has very strong views on most things, is a huge enthusiast, and joined the Grenadier Guards on leaving school. David, on the other hand, started rebelling many years before he could even spell the word. He had very blond curly hair which grew to halfway down his back as soon as he left school and was what I call a 'proper' hippy in the late sixties – a very exotic brother for a fifteen-year-old to have. He took the whole thing quite seriously and even spent six months at Her Majesty's pleasure for apparently dealing cannabis. He said it was for his own consumption – an entirely feasible argument in my view, but the judge wasn't convinced. This put my parents under a lot of strain and I remember feeling desperately sorry for them.

I sailed along quite calmly and quietly behind the maelstrom my brothers created ahead of me and learnt how to keep out of most trouble – feeling my parents probably had enough on their hands most of the time. It was wonderful having such diverse influences and I slipped very comfortably between them as I grew up. It fascinates me how fully formed one is as a person by about eighteen and I don't think my fundamental views, beliefs or take on people have changed much since then. Nature versus nurture has always been an interesting debate and, particularly looking at my children, I think it's about 50/50. You pop out into the world with a huge amount of your character in place; however, it is definitely influenced by your upbringing and I am sure you 'take colour' from those around you.

Thanks to a subsidy by the army we all went to boarding school from the age of eight. This was how it was, part of life, and we just got on with it. I went to Milton Abbey, a very impressive building with an abbey attached to it in beautiful countryside in Dorset. It was easy to get into and was not known for its academic flair. Whether we were thick because we just were, or because we were so badly taught I don't know, but it never worried us and I enjoyed my time there, regardless of being taught virtually nothing.

Despite this private 'education' (I use the word cautiously) we never had any money as a family and so lived extremely frugally. It could well have something to do with my parents having been brought up during the war and rationing, but suffice it to say that with one chicken to feed seven of us, it wasn't difficult to 'eat what's on your plate' as most children are instructed to do. Everything was done on a shoestring and holidays were spent either at home or, on more exotic occasions, in a caravan and tent. To this day my mother is incapable of spending money, will walk everywhere rather than take a tube, let alone a taxi, and every scrap of food is 'recycled' and destined to appear back in another dish some-time soon. The words health and safety hadn't been invented when we were growing up, which is just as well, as any modern-day inspector would have had a cardiac arrest if they had spent more than five minutes in our kitchen. I have a strong memory of rusty-lidded jars and the need to 'just scrape the mould off – it will be fine'. Needless to say, none of us were ever ill and we all have strong constitutions, no doubt due to our 'high bacteria' diet.

I had a very interesting conversation with my mother a few years ago, talking about my father's career in the army and was fascinated to hear that when I was eight years old and we were living in Hong Kong, his regiment had been merged with another. This resulted in him reporting to a senior officer from the other regiment. My father had always been very popular with all the soldiers under his command and, perhaps jealous of this, this senior officer took against him and made life difficult for him. The end result, and final act of vindictiveness, was for my father to be passed over for promotion, as this had to be sanctioned by his senior officer. My father was always extremely mild mannered, but apparently became more difficult to live with after this incident. And I can understand exactly why – particularly for him, as his father had been a well-known officer in the regiment and fought in both world wars, winning the VC in the First World War (it is also quite possible that his senior officer was resentful of this background). I was fascinated to hear this story, as I was not aware of it at the time, but wonder if I didn't get wind of it, or overhear conversations relating to it. I have an extreme sensitivity to people being abused in any way by those in a position of power, and wonder if it may not stem from a latent understanding of my father's predicament all those years ago. It is also quite possible that this influenced my determination not to rely on others myself.

A brief word about my grandfather at this point, as he has been a huge influence on me and the rest of my family. He not only survived the ordeals of the First World War, but fought in the Second, spending two years on the run in France before being smuggled by the Resistance to Spain and by boat back to England (even the boat voyage being inter-rupted by an attack from German planes). He finally got back to England and was able to make a telephone call home after two whole years of silence: 'Hello, it's George.' It's hard to imagine how emotional it must have been, although amazingly, my grandmother had always refused to accept he had been killed, to the point where she refused to take his pension which would only be given if a death certificate was signed. She later on refused to believe that God wouldn't cure her of cancer, being a committed Christian Scientist, and she died, having had no treatment, when I was two. You certainly can't fault her for lack of character, but it's a shame I didn't know her better as she sounds the most wonderful, slightly chaotic, undomesticated, 'door always open to everyone', friendly person. My grandfather re-married and finally died peacefully at home aged eighty-two. He left fascinating diaries, written at the time, in the most unemotional, factual style, but never talked about his experiences to us in any detail. He was a lovely grandfather to us and we used to stay with him for half terms and short Easter holidays throughout the time my parents were abroad. He always used very understated language and things may often have been 'a bit inconvenient' or 'a nuisance' but never 'an absolute nightmare' or 'complete disaster' or any of the other hysterical words we are now in the habit of using so liberally. I never once heard him raise his voice.

Whenever I have found life a bit tricky I have always used him as my reference – and once you have read a bit about life in the trenches on the Front Line, it becomes quite hard to complain too much.

In summary then, a fear of being treated badly by people above me, either through an understanding of my father's experience, or perhaps simply my own strong sense of right and wrong. A fear of not having enough money, because as a family we never had much, married to the view that with money comes options in life and ultimately, freedom. To be able to do what you want, when (and where) you want.

Life before Daily Bread: The City Years

So, a brief explanation as to how I ended up working for myself. After leaving the army, my eldest brother worked for a commodity broker, ED&F Man, and when they offered me a job I accepted it. This went against all my principles at the time – I was, after all, meant to be starting my career as a hippy, following my other brother, at least for a couple of years, but I decided to chase the buck instead. This was a huge decision as, from the age of about fifteen I had dreamed of little else but bucking the system and living a life full of peace and love and very loud rock music. 'Goa here I come,' except that I couldn't afford the airfare . . . Incidentally, deep down, I was never quite sure how successful I might have been at this. I used to spend a lot of my late teens at a school friend's house, a lovely rambling farmhouse in Ewhurst with a very bohemian feel to it. We had some wonderful times there, but as time went on it became more and more full of people that I increasingly came to think of as freeloaders lying around in a stupor mumbling 'hey man' while Hawkwind blasted out. 'There must be more to this hippy business than this,' I thought. I was nineteen and without any money and desperate to be independent, and that would have to take priority. First of all, however, the big commitment; I had to cut my hair – and there could be no greater sign of commitment in 1973 than that.

Changing tack so dramatically – replacing my T shirt and

flared jeans for a suit, and commuting up to the City every day – didn't come easily to me and I wrestled with this for some time. If there is one simple belief that I clung to then, and has remained with me since, it is that the power, and therefore attraction, of money is the freedom it brings. But it did mean compromising, and I clearly remember the alien feeling of trudging across London Bridge on a grey morning with hundreds of fellow commuters like so many ants going about their business.

Working at ED&F Man was, in fact, quite fun. They were a nice bunch of people, with a good sense of humour, and I really did enjoy the freedom it gave me. As it turned out, they would be easily the best company I ever worked for. Within a year I was renting a house with friends in London, had bought a car and was up and running. Two years later and an opportunity came up for two people to volunteer to work late to keep the office open while New York was trading. I took this up, was paid more, and was given a company car. This enabled me to get a mortgage and buy a small house. So far, so good, although I also knew that I was still on a totally mercenary trail, and would never be a real high flier as the work didn't captivate me in any way. This raises a fascinating question, I believe: can one make a real success of a career in a business one isn't really interested in? I don't think so. You can certainly get by – and many (most?) people do just that, but I believe you need to totally immerse yourself and be dedicated to the cause to push yourself and your company to be better than anyone else. I also believe that you have to aspire to being the best in your field, and so one of the main criteria when setting up a business is establishing how you are going to be the best. It doesn't matter what the business is, and it doesn't need to end up being big, but HOW can it be the best? And if it isn't, why would anyone ever use it?

I was keen to make money, but couldn't throw myself wholeheartedly at commodity trading. Was this because I was stupid, idle or just not fully engaged? I don't know, but I lean towards the latter.

After five years with Man trading sugar I was getting itchy feet and was worried that I might spend the rest of my working life there and look back at sixty and that would have been that. Somehow life had to be a bit more exciting than that. I decided to leave and try my hand at importing cement from Nigeria with a friend who had contacts in Lagos; ensuring supply would not be a problem, but we couldn't get an ECGD (Export Credit Guarantee Department) permit for our initial small order, and without this we ended up not shipping a single tonne. A wasted year later, I returned to commodities and, wanting to keep moving forward, got a job with Rayner Harwill, a small subsidiary of J. H. Rayner. Rayner Harwill was run by a couple of delightful guys, which is more than could ever be said for the parent company. Seeing how some of the senior staff working there were treated imbedded in me an intense determination not to be in a similar position when I was older. They were in their forties, children at school and absolutely couldn't afford to lose their jobs – and didn't the company just know it. I also had a pretty shitty job, my main client being a deeply unpleasant and demanding character who would scream if not updated exactly on the hour every hour with the latest prices. I had to take his pretty constant abuse as I needed the job to pay my mortgage, and so were sown some of the main seeds of my determination to be independent. It had been a big error joining the company and a humbling experience after the comparative comfort of working for a really decent company like Man.

Raynor Harwill closed down two years later and, as a

twenty-seven-year-old without a job, and having saved about £1000, I took the opportunity to go to Australia where I spent nine happy months doing manual work in Sydney and being a 'jackaroo' cowboy for a month mustering cattle on a ranch near Brisbane – one of the most enjoyable months of my life. I lived alone in a house on the ranch and acted as a gofer and an extra pair of hands to the manager and his two assistants. We all got on really well, and days were spent rounding up cattle and galloping after those that made a run for it, thundering in between trees in the woods or across vast open terrain playing catch me if you can, and nights often alone, or having dinner with the other hands. Eating in their houses was a brilliant experience and like something out of a film. We would start by playing pool, then have a huge steak, then one of the family would start playing the piano while the others sang country and western songs. Truly happy evenings. I think I ate steak every night for a month, and that was just fine by me.

However, despite some wonderful times, there remained this sneaking uncertainty as to what was going to happen next, and how I would support myself. In Australia I had lived off my labouring jobs and the savings I had made in London. I had rented my house out which just covered the mortgage and would very happily have stayed longer in Australia, but couldn't find a 'proper' job and so returned to England and, stupidly, returned to the only thing I knew a little about which was commodity broking. I started working for Cargill but before long took up a position at IG Index. IG is a financial bookmaker, enabling people to place bets on the future price of most commodities or shares – the big advantage for clients over trading through a commodity or stock broker is that any gains are tax-free. The work was tedious beyond words and became, for me, soul destroying. I spent most of my day endlessly answering the phone giving clients the latest price of gold or silver or the FTSE before putting the phone down or, occasionally, placing a bet for them. The company was run by Stuart Wheeler. Stuart was extremely bright, and also a very nice person to work for; however, he was not big on praise. I remember one occasion in particular when we had had a record month. Everyone was very excited by this and thrilled to tell Stuart when he returned from holiday. His reaction was completely muted and he simply asked what we were estimating to do for the following month. This had quite a profound effect on me and I determined that if I was ever in charge of a company, I would always make an effort to show my appreciation to staff if they did a good job.

After a couple of years, and with me becoming increasingly frustrated, Stuart took me to one side and suggested it might be a good idea if I looked for another job. I was sacked! He was quite right to do this. I was only there because I didn't have a clue what else to do, and worse than that, was fast running out of any energy or inspiration to do anything about it myself. Now the days of endless frustration and despondency were going to come to an end whether I liked it or not – and possibly only to be replaced by poverty and despondency. Not much of an upgrade really . . .

I had come to realise that I couldn't keep on complaining about the companies I worked for and that the time had come to work for myself. The problem was that after ten years of being a (not terribly good) commodity broker/book maker I didn't really know how to do anything else. The City is a shocking apprenticeship for almost any other kind of work, and so I found myself, at the age of thirty-one, with a small house, a mortgage to pay, no money and no job. It was time for action.

Employment up to this point had been primarily just a means to an end, to live off, and I only realised when I set up my own business how important it is to really get engaged in your work. People around me in the City made quite good money at this time, but I never did and, to be fair, I didn't deserve to. It was also an interesting lesson in how it just takes one or two wrong decisions (like returning to commodity trading when I came back from Australia) to have a dramatic effect on one's life.

One right decision can also have a huge effect, and the best thing about my time at IG Index is that I met my wife, Harriet, there and we became engaged at around the time I left the company. I am intrigued at the twists and turns that life throws up and IG Index taught me finally (I was always a slow learner) that I should give up my City career. It also provided me with a fantastic wife – and you can't ask more of a company than that.

I was given three months notice and so had time to look around at what possible options I had. It wasn't a pretty picture. A particular low point was going to see a headhunter friend of my father-in-law to be. The company my father-in-law worked for had been a loyal client of his, recruiting staff through him for many years, and so I turned up in his West End office with a certain degree of optimism. I was feeling pretty low at this time and could have done with a little perking up – maybe a few suggestions of alternative careers or opportunities. Instead I had the most dispiriting meeting of my life. As he sat back in his chair rubbishing my CV, he couldn't have been more dismissive and less helpful, and I remember leaving his office after about twenty minutes with a determination that, one day, I would show him. I am a firm believer that all these experiences help fuel the fire of ambition, but at the time all I felt was pure anger – a dog that had been kicked when it was down. I remember being asked by my in-laws how the meeting had gone. 'Not terribly well,' I said, feeling I couldn't give them the full vent of my fury. 'Oh yes, well, he can be a bit eccentric,' they said. Too bloody right.

So, I had to think of something, but didn't really know where to start. If I was going to set something up, it would have to need very little capital (I had about £1000 in savings) and be able to turn a profit very quickly.

I left IG Index in early 1986. At this time there was one good small chain of sandwich bars in the City named Birley's. At their shops delicious sandwiches were made to order in front of you on gleaming marble by staff in stiff white uniforms. It was a class act and very popular. IG Index was based in Victoria, where the only sandwiches available were from traditional Italian Mom and Pop shops or, much worse, British Rail at the station. And so the idea began to form in my mind that it might be possible to start a business making similar sandwiches to Birley's and taking them round local offices. The advantages of this model as I saw it were that I didn't have the money or the experience to open my own shop and, more excitingly, there wouldn't be a restriction on numbers. The problem with a shop making bespoke sandwiches is that you only have a reasonably short period of time to make them. There is only so much counter space, and so sales are always going to be limited. By making in bulk the sky was the limit, or at least something like that.

CHAPTER 1

How *Not* to Start a Business

'We learn wisdom from failure much more than from success. We often discover what will do, by finding out what will not do; and probably he who never made a mistake never made a discovery.' Samuel Smiles.

On the basis that you can learn as much from negatives as positives, listen up, because I almost created a master class in How Not To Do It.

Patience has never been a strong point of mine, and starting Daily Bread couldn't have been a better example of this characteristic in full flow. I'm not sure where this impatience comes from, but to this day it shows no sign of going away and I am almost certain that I could spend three months on a Caribbean beach and *still* be driven mad having to wait more than thirty seconds for my midday cocktail at the beach bar. I am often referred to as Jeremy (as in Paxman) by my family when I've shouted 'C'mon' for the umpteenth time as we try and leave the house. While not always a good thing, I still however maintain that, provided it is controlled, it is overall a good characteristic; when you have a lot of bases to cover, you just can't afford to hang around.

To start with, it's hard to imagine anyone less suited to setting up a food business of any sort than me. I'm not a foodie in any shape – quantity has, until very recently, been just as important as quality to me, and I don't cook because it doesn't interest me at all and I regard it as a waste of time.

I also didn't have a clue about running a business of any sort, as the City is good training for nothing at all but the City. I did know what a good sandwich tasted like. The one over-riding thing about food, however, was that it was a repeat business – you didn't need to constantly find a new customer for every product you sold and, not being a good salesman myself, this was extremely attractive. Provided it was good enough, whoever bought a sandwich today might well buy another tomorrow. The other huge factor was that it cost almost nothing to set up and could, possibly, make money from day one.

So, no market research, no visiting offices in advance to see if they would like a basket round in their office. No experience in running a business, let alone catering, no idea of what margins to aim for. In fact, no idea how to start at all. The back-of-a-fag-packet calculation that I did go to the trouble of making was that, if I could make and sell a hundred sandwiches a day, I should be able to make 50p profit a sandwich which would be £250 profit a week, which was not bad, and certainly sufficient in those days.

My advice to anyone setting up a business would be to gain some experience in the best company they can find in the sector they are interested in first, and then work out how they can do it better. There is so much to learn and it is so much better to learn from others' experience – and expense. So why didn't I? I think age played a big part, as well as pride. I was thirty-one and setting up one's own sandwich delivery business was one thing, going to work for a sandwich manufacturer was quite another and besides, what was I going to be able to offer them? Another reasonable point was that there was no other company delivering sandwiches to offices as I planned to – just the odd girl working from her flat, and my idea was to try and start a professional version.

The other reason would once again be impatience; I was keen to just get cracking and couldn't wait. After all, what could be complicated about it?

I saw a friend who worked in PR at a party and told him I was thinking of setting up a sandwich delivery business and was wondering what to call it. Quick as a flash he came up with Soldiers, Use Your Loaf and Daily Bread. Daily Bread immediately sounded right and the decision was instant. I could straight away imagine answering the phone with the name and that was that.

David Mathewson was an old friend that I had met when I first moved to London and we had shared a house together with two others. David had qualified as a chartered accountant and kindly offered to help me set up Daily Bread in his spare time. His help was selfless and amazing and essential and, not being able to afford to pay him, I offered him 10 per cent of the business for which he paid £10. I never regretted doing this and when we parted company 12 years later he received a healthy return on his investment.

I did also enrol the support of a friend, Kate Slessor and she had 30 per cent of the company. We lent the company £800 to buy baskets, a meat slicer and some cutting boards and knives and off we went.

The first thing we did was to hold a tasting party at my house and make up a mass of sandwiches and get some reaction to them. I remember it being *so* much harder than we thought, and particularly when you are trying to make a few for the first time, and you know they are going to be closely inspected. Apart from anything else, the difficulty of spreading cold butter on bread had to be overcome. The tiny kitchen in my house also looked like a bomb had hit it, but I was more used to that. The day went pretty well, with lots of compliments, but this is the problem with such an exercise –

it's very hard for people to be too critical when they don't want to be discouraging. An interesting thing did come out of this period: one of my best friends told me he thought I was mad and had lost my senses. Wandering around offices selling sandwiches, at your age? I appreciated and admired his honesty and was discussing this with him recently when I explained how motivating I had found his comments. I guess it can go either way, and many is the person that has been helped to achieve great things through the support and encouragement of a particular teacher at school, or a mentor of some kind. Equally, there are many that have been spurred on by being told that they would never amount to anything. Whilst the latter is obviously never to be recommended, I suspect that the reality is that 'negative inspiration' is often a factor in the drive behind successful people. I do also believe that there is a certain insecurity behind almost all successful people, some deep-seated need to push themselves and prove themselves above others.

A friend of my younger brother owned The Pieman deli in Chelsea Green and I agreed a rent of ten sandwiches a day for an unused kitchen in the basement below. If there's one thing I most dislike doing, it's getting up early in the morning – the only exception being getting up early to go on holiday, and even then it can be a close run thing. I just hate it. The first day started at 4.30am. Kate and I cooked a chicken, some sausages and bacon, stripping the chicken while it was still too hot to really handle and made our first fifty sandwiches. We stuck to the standard sandwich menu of the time, but doing 'premium' versions as had been pioneered by Birley's, and including BLT, ham salad, chicken salad, sausage and tomato, egg mayo and cress, and bacon and avocado. Having no idea where to buy wholesale ingredients, we bought every-thing from Sainsbury's including eggs which we had to boil and peel before cutting up to make the egg mayo. I had borrowed my mother's Renault 5 and by about 11am we both had a basket full of cling-film wrapped sandwiches and we headed off to Victoria to see if we could find some suitable office blocks to walk round. It is amazing how much has changed in the years since then, as we could walk into almost any office and only had to talk our way past the receptionist (it would be almost impossible to start a similar business in central London nowadays for this reason). From the first day, a strong sense of optimism was essential and if we were rejected by one office, it was straight onto the next one to try our luck. One of the things I most liked was that I felt we were offering something that was really good and people would want it if we could just get it to them, and so the odd battleaxe that kicked us out was doing the staff in the building as much a disservice as us. It was essential to have such a sense of optimism and confidence in the sandwiches and I continued to maintain this attitude throughout the following years. Kate and I had gone in different directions in Victoria, and met up again by the car at about 1.30. I think we had both sold just over half of our baskets and sold a total of thirty-five that day before returning to the kitchen to wash up the greasy cooking pans, count the money, buy more food for the next day, and collapse. It was 10th March 1986 and at least Daily Bread was born, and we were up and running.

After the concern and uncertainty of the previous few months it was quite a relief to be underway with a new venture and what I most recall is the great feeling of working in a 'real' business. Making and selling something was fantastic and felt more 'pure' than earning a living shifting paper around as I had for the past ten years.

Kate and I continued this routine for the next two months, slowly increasing our rounds and growing bit by bit. It was hard, grinding, work and quite physically tiring, but each day we sold a few more, and that was a great feeling.

As soon as we had a round up to about seventy sandwiches we found a friend, or more often, a friend of a friend, to take it over and paid them a percentage of the takings for the round. This acted as a great temporary job for them and a good way of earning a bit of cash for a few hours work. We would then spend our time developing new rounds. Pat had helped clean my house during my days of gainful employment, and after a few weeks she came in to help us make sandwiches. Once Pat was settled in, after about three months, Kate decided she'd had enough and wanted to leave. I didn't blame her at all, as it was nothing but a hard, and not terribly rewarding, slog. I paid her back the £30 she had paid for her shares and any money she had lent the company and, although I missed her, it was in a way easier being able to make decisions by myself and feel completely in control.

Every day felt like a rush against the clock. We had to get the sandwiches made by latest 10am to get the baskets out in time for the lunch period. We were now going round offices in Pimlico and Victoria and slowly built up round by round with the basket sellers either getting round on foot, having been dropped off by me, or in their own car.

While all this was going on I was due to be getting married in October and Harriet had mentioned we should perhaps sell my house and her flat and get somewhere together. 'Fair enough,' I said, rather absent-mindedly but was quite surprised when a couple of days later I returned home to find an estate agent waiting by my door. This girl doesn't hang about, I thought to myself and, while a bit stunned, I was equally impressed by her speed of action. This was something I was to get used to and I'm now quite surprised if things at home *don't* happen immediately.

One of things that most amazes me about this period was that we not only moved house and got married, but also managed to go on honeymoon for a week in Turkey. And this was just over six months after starting the business. Life was a blur but we seemed to manage to juggle everything, and I was probably most impressed with my parents-in-law for accepting me in the way they did. I just thanked God I didn't have to go through one of those 'and so what are your prospects, young man?' conversations, because it would have been quite a brief chat.

My abiding memory of this time was rushing around from office to office, always hoping not to get a parking ticket while inside one. One ticket would easily wipe out the profit from that round and I grew to dislike parking wardens with a vengeance. It was somehow more personal than getting a ticket if you were chancing it while going shopping. One of the offices I naturally went round was IG Index and they were always full of support. It was always a bit strange carrying a basket into an office where you knew the people, and occasionally I would bump into someone I had met socially, but everyone was always encouraging. I remember a friend that got me into Citibank's offices in Aldwych and will always appreciate how helpful he was and how he would always exhort all those around him to buy a sarnie when I came round. We had some great people working for us doing the original rounds through our little network, often just for one or two months, and the little basement kitchen became more and more busy. A particular highlight was finally buying a tiny Suzuki micro van. This was a very professional move and it started to feel like a proper business, even though it remained very hand to mouth. We also made the big decision at this point to put labels on our sandwiches, mainly to help any new basket seller know what was what and also the prices, as well as starting to promote our name. I asked a friend of my brother-in-law who did some design work, and for a nominal amount he came up with a banner design which we were to use for the next fifteen years. This was done in blue which at the time was almost unheard of for a food company – the standard colours of food brands at the time were a pale brown or orange colour, but they seemed pretty dull to me, so I thought we'd be different and have something a bit more lively. We had no computer and so we had to buy sheets of labels, write on them by hand, and then go to Prontaprint to have them copied. The sandwiches were still wrapped in cling-film – never the smartest packaging, but they really were excellent and huge care went into making every one. I was a pretty useless sandwich maker, mainly because I cared too much and each one had to be perfect – at least that was the excuse I always gave myself for going so slowly. Thinking of this: Beware the perfectionist. It is a word that I can't stand and I would never employ someone that cited it as one of their key competences. In my experience it is too often used as an excuse to endlessly faff about and never actually finish anything.

The kitchen also looked like a bomb had gone off whenever I was anywhere near it. The hardest part for me was back pain. I'm 6ft tall, and standing and leaning over a table really hurt me after a few hours. The benefit I gleaned from this had a lasting and important influence on how I ran the company, and I have always had huge respect for all our kitchen staff, knowing exactly how hard their work is.

We found a supplier of delicious honey-cooked ham and rare roast beef, and he delivered to us once a week, with us slicing them on our meat slicer, our most valuable asset at the time. My mother also made an incredible apple and walnut chutney which we used for the cheddar sandwiches.

Otherwise I bought our salad from Fry's, the greengrocer next door, and, increasingly from an excellent food wholesaler run by a friend of mine. An interesting point here: we always paid the full price to this company and never received a discount – even a small gesture would have been nice, particularly as we were just getting going. I had naturally asked, but was told their prices were their prices and that was that. A few years later, when we were much bigger and had started really negotiating with our suppliers, we extracted substantial discounts from them and if they couldn't match the price on anything with another supplier we would use that supplier. We have continued to use them to this day, and they have always given us a great service, but I ended up being grateful for their slightly hard-nosed approach at the beginning as it enabled me not to feel any loyalty to them and, over the years, we saved a fortune by shopping around. Business would be business, and that was fine with me.

CHAPTER 2

Our Own Place

After a year I decided to make the big move to our own premises and found a small industrial unit just south of the river in Sleaford Street – by coincidence right next door to New Covent Garden where we finally ended up many years later. We had had quite a good year from a standing start, and we turned over £85k in our first full year.

The unit was 500 sq ft and I built a mezzanine over a quarter of it to provide an office upstairs. This was quite a commitment, as it was on a five-year lease from Wandsworth Council. We had a large walk-in fridge, an oven (second hand from somewhere), a sink and a stainless steel table in the middle with a kitchen worktop around the sides. It was very exciting moving into our own space and having more room – it had become increasingly difficult negotiating the tight spiral staircase from the Pieman's basement, laden with baskets and crates of sandwiches, as well as having to feed parking meters all the time we were there.

The downside was that we didn't have proper extraction from the oven and so, while it provided some nice heat during the winter, we became fumigated from the smoke from burning bacon fat and it was sometimes almost un-bearable. Another, smaller but important issue was getting the butter at the right temperature. A few seconds too long in the oven and you had a yellow soup, too few and it wasn't spreadable. Everything was incredibly basic and friends still remind us of when we would stay with them for the weekend, and on Sunday morning we would produce a huge case of eggs and have to cook them on the Aga and then shell them, ready for Monday's production. It was a few years before we were able to buy such things ready made and it's incredible how much easier so many things are now. Even forms of communication we take completely for granted now didn't exist at the time, so no mobiles or emails, and we were positively showing off when we finally bought a fax machine, let alone our first computer.

We had about five or six rounds going by this stage and had expanded into the West End, going round quite a few offices in Berkeley Square and its vicinity. We also started taking more and more orders for platters of sandwiches that offices were ordering for meetings. We had cardboard boxes made to put the platters in and make stacking them easy. These had our logo on and looked really neat. It was also copied from the way Birley's delivered their platters.

The main problem we started encountering was staff reliability. We had four people now working in the kitchen, but if just one of them didn't turn up, then we were short of 25 per cent of our workforce, let alone if two of them were away at the same time.

Quite often we would recruit someone, and they would leave before the day was even out claiming it was too hard work. Alternatively they just didn't turn up the following day, so we never knew what would face us each day we arrived for work. We were starting at about 6am now that we had become a little more organised and if anyone didn't turn up either in the kitchen or for doing a round, then I would step in and trying to find new rounds would have to take a backseat. I remember employing a young guy who had been working at a small sandwich shop in Victoria called Prêt a

Manger (they started by coincidence the same year as us) and him saying how well organised we were compared to them, which just goes to show what amazing progress they made as, about four years later, Prêt suddenly exploded on the High Street as one of the most disciplined and well-managed companies there are.

1987 was a huge year; I had moved the business to our own premises, and Harriet and I sold our properties and bought a house in Stockwell, mainly for its large garden, although it needed quite a bit of work done on it. As a result we were staying with a friend while it was done up and then, to cap it all, Harriet announced she was pregnant. What a wonderful, lovely surprise, and the race was now on as to whether the house would be ready by the time the baby arrived. It quite soon became apparent that having a heavily pregnant wife dealing with builders was not a good idea, particularly if we wanted the house to remain standing, and so I spent a lot of time rushing from work to the house and back again and we finally moved in just before the BIG day.

At around this time my brother-in-law Graham (my sister's husband) came to work with me. He had been a picture framer but the company he worked for had got into difficulties and he initially joined me just to help out. He was exactly the pair of hands I needed, being extremely practical and also very charming and therefore a very popular sandwich seller. He soon became very involved and took over the day-to-day running of the basket sales while I concentrated on sales of platters for meetings and the rest of the business. There was a limit to how many staff we could have working due to the size of the unit and so we had to start earlier and earlier as we became more busy. Sometimes we were inevitably late due to a late starter or a no-show and that started to affect the ability of the basket sellers to do their job properly and earn the money they needed. By this point we were selling not only sandwiches but also drinks, crisps and brownies (from a company run by a Canadian called Bourne St Brownies. They were the best brownies I've ever had and, somehow, impossible to replicate – she kept the recipe a closely guarded secret unfortunately, and when she returned to Canada her recipe went with her). If we ran too late with production we felt duty bound to subsidise the sandwich sellers when they subsequently had a bad day and this became expensive after a while.

The decision was then made to make during the night, rather than start early in the morning. The main advantages of this were that we would always have time on our side, and also that it would be easier for any kitchen staff without cars to get to work. It was also taking longer and longer to load each seller's basket with their exact order. There was a natural concern about the possible effect on freshness, but we reckoned the advantages outweighed this, and it was very hard to tell any difference in quality. We also bought an Amstrad computer, which was a huge breakthrough as everything had been done by hand up to that point. We could now collate the basket seller's orders onto a single spreadsheet to produce a production sheet for the total number of each sandwich to be produced the following day, rather than adding them up by hand. We also devised a spreadsheet showing the value of each order and could compare this with the takings from the round. Inevitably, takings didn't match sales when regular customers were given credit (always with the basket seller's promise that it would be made up very soon) and so Graham had to keep a complex record of each round's shortages. £1.50 short one day, £2.25 the next, and soon we were £30 out of pocket. Of course if the seller left suddenly, we were stuffed, and this happened a few times, but we were so busy keeping the wheels spinning, and, most importantly, being keen not to alienate the sellers that we accepted the risk. If a seller left not only would Graham have to cover their round – and me too if we were two down – but then have to deal with all the other daily routine as well as finding a new seller and training them in how to do the round. Most of our business was now in the City and West End, but if a new seller had never been to the City before, it was quite intimidating and easy to get lost, or forget how to get to the next office. It was worth trying to keep the existing sellers happy at almost any cost. While building up more rounds, and encouraging the sellers to try and increase their own rounds, Graham had started recruiting 'resting' actors as they had exactly the credentials necessary to be a good sandwich seller, being naturally outgoing and keen to 'perform'. It was always interesting how the ones with the best character and wit would consistently outsell the others, and this was much more important than their appearance. Most of them really enjoyed the work and enjoyed it more if they knew their regulars and could have a bit of banter with them each day. We had some great characters and some would become positively poetic in their descriptions of our sarnies – an egg and cress sandwich could easily become 'hand-chopped freshly laid eggs lovingly laid to rest on a bed of the finest mustard cress in between two slices of the healthiest possible granary bread'.

In our second year we turned over £188k and gathered a bit of momentum, but it was still very much hand to mouth and I was just making enough to survive. Graham provided a safe and reliable pair of hands and did a great job in developing the basket rounds and was by now working with us full time. We would periodically go to the pub on a Friday night with some of the sellers to celebrate the end of the week, and that was always a good evening.

During the start of our third year, I stumbled across something that had quite an effect on how I viewed the business. We had set out to sell-top quality sandwiches direct to offices; however, the reality is that not everyone wanted the absolute best, they wanted something that was good and reliable sold to them by someone pleasant in a convenient way – and what could be more convenient than being served at your desk. We were still buying gallon jars of apple and walnut chutney from my mother, but she had gone on holiday and we had run out. The ingredients were costing her around £4.50 and I paid her £6 per jar. We now bought most of our basic ingredients from the cash and carry across the road from us, and I would generally do a weekly shop there. I ended up buying a gallon jar of family value sweet pickle for £2.50 to see how we got on with it as an emergency. No one said a single word and I realised that what I thought the customer wanted and the reality were not the same thing. This was a huge lesson – don't ever assume you know what your customers want, because you could be busting a gut to provide something way in excess of their expectation. I'm not criticising having quality at the forefront of any business, but a good, healthy commercial eye is also just as important, and the world is littered with the carcasses of food businesses that have produced the most amazing goods, but at the detriment of being commercially viable.

Incidentally, my mother had enjoyed helping out and being involved, but was also quite relieved not to have her small kitchen overrun by sticky chutney production any more.

At around this time, in reply to an advert in the local paper, William arrived. William was from France and was exactly what we needed – totally reliable and dedicated and he remained with us running the kitchen for the next five years along with his less dynamic, but equally dedicated cousin Pascal. I am conscious of having used the word reliable quite often in writing this, but for any small business it is obviously critical and it is not easily found in a business that relies on manual labour as we did. One of the main lessons learnt over the following years was endlessly trying to refine the art of staff motivation (and, on occasions, self-motivation) and build a team of people who felt a strong sense of loyalty to each other as well as to the company. One of the main advantages of growing and having more staff, is that you become less vulnerable to just a few individuals. In the early days we were forced to compromise on far too many occasions for fear of losing someone when they should have been disciplined or even sacked.

We were taking more orders for platters and would accept orders up until 11am for the same day's lunchtime delivery. Quite a service, and quite a nightmare. I hate letting people down, and felt we would always only be as good as our last delivery and that if we screwed up, that client wouldn't use us again. As a result our little Suzuki had to scream around London trying desperately to get to offices in time for their meetings. There were no mobile phones, and so once the van had left it was out of contact. There was always a huge time pressure, and I had one classic Basil Fawlty moment when I had set off late and in a rush in the van to make some deliveries. We could get two of our platter boxes in a baker's crate and I had about five crates stacked on top of each other in the back of the van. Driving past Battersea Dogs home and turning right to go up to Chelsea Bridge, I took the corner too fast and heard an almighty crash in the back. I stopped the van to find crumpled boxes and sandwiches lying all over the back, and picked up one of the now empty crates and hurled it with all my might across the road in utter fury.

Even when deliveries went smoothly, there was the still the fear of parking and getting tickets while you were making the delivery, and our tickets amounted to hundreds of pounds each year. The one fantastic exception to this was No 10 Downing Street where not only was parking laid on, but you also had someone to open the door for you – the perfect client! An old friend of mine was a secretary to Margaret Thatcher and she rang one day and asked if we might do a platter of sandwiches for her boss. We subsequently continued to supply them periodically up until the day she resigned. We even made a delivery on that day, and I resisted the temptation to ring up a paper and say that every cloud has a silver lining and, although she had had a terrible day, at least she'd had a great sandwich. Most of the deliveries we made were paid for by Conservative Central Office, but one, for the princely sum of £12.05, was paid by Mrs Thatcher herself. Reasoning that the cheque itself was worth more than the sum it was drawn for, I kept it and had it framed.

The business slowly developed and turnover had reached £250k by the following year. This was OK, but all my focus remained on getting through each day and each week. We still had masses of small issues to deal with and it was very rare to have a regular straightforward day when we didn't have a problem with production, not having enough staff or running out of one ingredient or another, or burning the bacon and having to start cooking again – always assuming that the oven was working OK. Graham showed amazing resilience through all of this and we were both often completely exhausted by the end of each day. While William was running the kitchen, and had about six people working with him, Graham and I were the spare pairs of hands and, despite our new night shift for production, we would still regularly have to help out making sandwiches to make sure they were ready on time. William would always ring me if there was an issue. Most memorably, I went to bed at 11pm one night having had a pretty busy day, and the phone rang at 11.05 with William telling me that three people hadn't turned up for work. I got out of bed, put my clothes back on and went in to make sandwiches all night and then carried on doing my usual work for the rest of the day. I naturally used to sometimes wonder what I was doing in this ridiculous business, but I never once regretted not being in the City. That was an exception, but William would regularly ring me to let me know that they were running behind or had run out of something and what should they replace it with, the worst part being that I often used to wake up in the middle of the night imagining the phone had rung even when it hadn't. Our unit was also burgled a few times during weekends and bits of cash and food taken. The worst part of it was the depressing feeling of being disrupted by some mindless yob. By the time we left the unit after five years it looked more like a prison camp than an industrial unit, with metal reinforcements on the doors and strengthened skylights to avoid them coming through the roof.

CHAPTER 3

Union Court

After about four years in Sleaford Street I had to start thinking about the next stage. The big decision was whether to carry on or not, as the end of the five-year lease would free me of any obligation, and if I was going to stop that would have been the perfect time. If we did carry on, we would need bigger premises and that would cost more. In an ideal world we would buy our own premises, but I had no cash for this. By this time we had two children and I was reluctant to risk everything by borrowing heavily against our house. I did decide, however, that, having put so much work into it, it would be a pity to throw it away. What helped make my mind up was a meeting I had with the catering company that looked after British Gas. We had supplied them with some platters, and they wondered if I would like to talk to them about supplying sandwiches to their staff restaurant as they were thinking of changing supplier. This was a business I never wanted to get into, my reasoning being that by selling directly to the end user we were maximising our margins, whereas we would have to give up quite a chunk of margin by wholesaling to a third party, and have to make a lot more sandwiches to make the same profit. I was tempted however, and a little flattered that they might think of using us, and any extra sales would be useful if we moved to larger premises. I went along to British Gas expecting to meet with the woman that had rung me for a bit of a chat, and immediately found myself facing a barrage of questions from five of her colleagues. The word 'unprepared' doesn't really cover it, and even my undoubted enthusiasm for the quality of our sandwiches wasn't going to swing it. It was quite a lesson, and I realised two things. One was that there was an interesting opportunity in the wholesale sector, and the other was that we would have to be a whole lot more professional if we were going to make any inroads into it.

After much searching, I came across a brand new industrial development, Union Court, in Lambeth and about 15 minutes' walk from our house. Close proximity to the house was important as I never knew when I would need to be at work in case of emergency. The unit was an empty shell and so we would have to kit it out from scratch. After much discussion with David we felt we could risk a loan of £100k, to be repaid over the following ten years. We took it on a ten-year lease and were given a year's rent free to help us settle in and also as an inducement as we were the first tenants on the estate. The loan was from Barclays, and I had no alternative but to put the house up as a personal guarantee. This was pretty scary, but would have been inevitable wherever we had gone. I employed David's brother-in-law as our architect and we set about planning the new unit. The unit had the benefit of being double height and so we were able to put in a mezzanine floor, which would have the advantage of doubling the space we could use for the same ground-floor rent. The ground floor was 2000sq ft and so we would be going from the 500sq ft we had at Sleaford Street to 4000sq ft of usable space. The difficulty was combining running the existing business while planning the new unit, and it was incredible the amount of decisions that had to be made. First of all the big things, such as the flow from storing ingredients through to loading the finished sandwiches, allowing for the layout of the drains and the general design of the building, and then on to every single power point, light etc., etc. It was a very hectic time, but it had to be done and we somehow got through it and I was very happy with the overall result. This time also neatly coincided with us having our third child. I don't know why it is, but there is some curious law that dictates that one must be moving into either a new home, or new business premises, at exactly the time a child is due.

We were now in a palace compared to our last unit; it was just a matter of having to pay for it all. It was now 1992 and the economy was beginning to go into what would become quite a prolonged recession. We of course didn't anticipate that happening, but many was the time over the next few years when I was so grateful not to have taken a big punt and bought our own unit. It would have been crippling trying to finance the debt to buy the premises *and* kit them out, with a business that wasn't growing and had much higher overheads. I have little doubt we would have gone bust if we had taken that route, and so I learnt the value of timing. I have come to the conclusion that almost everything ultimately hinges on timing. This not only applies to decisions you can make, but also to when you meet people that have an influence on your life, all the way through to when you pop your clogs. It's also probably the part of life, apart from health, that requires the most luck.

I recognised sales as our weak point if we wanted to make progress in the wholesale world, and employed various sales-men during our time at Union Court, none of whom could really make much progress, and I would eventually have to ask them to leave. It's difficult to know why we had such a struggle employing someone in this role. OK, it wasn't the most glamorous industry, and to be working out of a small industrial estate in South London isn't everyone's idea of an ambition fulfilled. We couldn't pay too much of course, so that wouldn't help, but even later on, even when we did chuck money at it, it still didn't work. My constant drive to push forward and barely concealed impatience probably didn't help, and on a deeper level I don't personally like being sold to, and maybe I employed people too much in my own mould. But of course they also didn't care about the business as much as I did, and that could easily irritate me. Ultimately I suspect the main problem was that I didn't manage them well. Setting strict targets and reviewing them all the time was not my style, but maybe that's what was needed. This turned out to be my Achilles' heel for the next 15 or so years – an endless quest for a really good salesman. And no, with the odd exception, I never found them, and so eventually embarked on a new strategy which was to produce such a good product and such a good service that they would sell themselves, but this would take some time.

After a year or so at Union Court William had to return home to France, his cousin Pascal having returned the year before. Two things come immediately to mind when I think of them. Firstly the sight of William's hands almost rubbed raw from peeling endless eggs – and him never complaining about that or anything else; and secondly, Pascal's perform-ance at our Christmas dinner one year. The kitchen staff decided they should meet up before dinner at a nearby pub. We had booked a small room in the basement of an Italian restaurant in Wandsworth Bridge Road, and by the time they arrived for dinner they were clearly well oiled, but in good spirits. Halfway through pudding Pascal stood up, raised his glass to the ceiling and, in his finest English, wished everyone a happy . . . and then passed out, collapsing onto the middle of the table, scattering plates, glasses and bottles everywhere. It was an outstanding exhibition, and particularly from a man who wouldn't normally say boo to a goose. He was devastated returning to work the following Monday and I had to console him and let him know that he had actually made, not ruined, our party that night.

It was a shame to lose William. He had worked really hard and held production together for the past few years; however, he was not a people person and, as we employed more staff, that increasingly became an issue. Through him going, someone else was given the opportunity to shine. And that someone else was the ultimate people person and was to end up having an incredible impact on the business. Seham Ahmedein was an Egyptian and had come over to England with her husband five years earlier, worked running a café, and when that closed had joined us the year before William left. I had very much left the running of the kitchen to William, but Seham had become more and more conspicuous and was the obvious person to take over from him. We were still making sandwiches through the night, but I would increasingly see Seham when she stayed on in the morning, dealing with one issue or another.

We pretty much broke even over the next two years and, while turnover increased up to £660k by 1994, our increased overheads meant our profit didn't grow – fortunately something we had allowed for in our budgeting – and so we were able to mark time and ride it out. It was wonderful being in so much better premises, and one that I wouldn't mind showing off to potential clients. I had by now also realised that any large client would automatically want to audit us and so this was essential. At least I now felt we could start approaching some bigger players in the wholesale market and see if we could supply them. The short answer was consistently 'No'. For a start no one knew who we were, and we also had no wholesale track record to show off about. Lastly, but probably most importantly, we weren't the cheapest, and that was more important than anything else at that time. At last I had a breakthrough and managed to start supplying a few sandwiches to the Stock Exchange. The catering was handled by a new company, Charlton House, and they liked the idea of having a different supplier from their competitors, and they were also more quality focused. I got on really well immediately with the unit manager who was a decent guy who didn't feel the need to throw his weight about, and we established a very good trading relationship. We had our first proper client.

I have to take my hat off to what Charlton House have gone on to achieve. They had just started at that time and are now one of the biggest independent contract caterers in the UK and with good reason, as they have been steadfast in their determination to provide genuinely good quality catering. As they grew, the managers of their new units came to like what we were about and they remained a very good and loyal client.

In the meantime, basket sales continued to grow . We had a lot more room to load baskets and soon had to buy a second van to handle the deliveries of platters.

The last couple of years had gone by quite quickly and it felt a lot of work for not much reward. The recession hadn't helped, and there was a general sense of everyone tightening their belts, so it was not the best market in which to be trying to promote a premium offer, even in sandwiches. Turnover had increased as we found more small wholesale clients and developed the basket rounds and platter sales, but we were only making a tiny profit on this and I was paying myself just enough to support myself and my family. We used every spare minute ringing up businesses, or simply walking the streets and going into offices trying to drum up new business, as well as going through the telephone directory and ringing any big-sounding companies in the right area. The problem with the basket sales business was that it was very bitty. Each round might generate £100–£120 total sales, but they were all individually small orders and it was very fiddly to load the exact orders into the baskets each morning. At our peak, we were running about 12 rounds, so this took quite a bit of work. Recruitment was also a recurring theme as very few basket sellers would work with us for more than a few months and so Graham was endlessly interviewing and training new ones. The platter orders were also beginning to take their toll, as the time pressure became too intense. The phones would be ringing the entire morning now, firstly with orders for that day's lunch meetings (and despite our attempts to get them to order the day before, there was still a mass of orders coming in on the day) and then, later on, from clients wondering where their order was and when was it going to be delivered: 'I've got 12 people sitting in a meeting room and one very angry boss wondering where their lunch is, what can you tell me?' We eventually decided to move the order cut-off time back to 10am to give us more time. We really were flying by the seat of our pants, and every day was a blur of activity, but we equally didn't want to say no to any business. This is a classic dilemma for any small business and it took some years before we had the confidence to decline new business if we felt we couldn't manage it really well.

At the Stock Exchange the orders had grown larger and larger and they were becoming a significant part of our business. Unfortunately the original unit manager was promoted to a new job elsewhere and I had his polar opposite to deal with. She was a young girl whose early morning sport was to find something to complain about and ring me up. Why? I guess because she could. I don't mind criticism at all, particularly if it's constructive, and I've often said subsequently that it is the good clients that complain – the others don't say anything and are likely to eventually stop using us. This, though, was just taking the piss. They were too big a client to upset, and so my hands were tied and I had to play along with it. It was becoming ever more important that we find some new wholesale business, as I hated the feeling of being reliant on a large client with a stroppy manager.

A couple of years later, when we were at our most vulnerable and in real trouble, and they were still our biggest client, I finally had had enough. I snapped on the phone and told her this and suggested she had better get another supplier if all she could do was criticise all the time. We were busting a gut to provide them with a great service, and all she could do was complain. I went home that evening thinking I had probably put the final nail in our coffin, but also quite relieved that I wouldn't be putting up with any more shit. As it turned out, they continued to use us and she was as good as gold from then on. Another lesson learnt.

By about 1994 I was really beginning to question what the whole thing was about. It seemed such hard work just to stand still and I was finding it harder and harder going into work. I was having to deal with any complaints first thing in the morning. These would typically be that the sandwiches had arrived late, the delivery had sandwiches missing, or had been left at the wrong place, or a quality issue of some sort, and then, often feeling pretty demoralised, I had to try and put my sales hat on and get ringing people to try and find new business for the rest of the day. On top of this were all the usual day-to-day issues with staff, or production issues that needed dealing with, and if it wasn't that, then the printer would break and we couldn't print any production sheets or labels for the next day's delivery. No labels meant we couldn't sell any sandwiches (those days had sadly gone, and it would be totally unacceptable not to have labels at this stage, and certainly with our wholesale business) and so a small problem could easily escalate to become a big one – and that was even before one of the vans broke down again . . . Part of our problem was that it was so hand to mouth, that all our equipment was old and left us permanently vulnerable. Of course, with the benefit of hindsight we should have borrowed some money and invested in newer and better machinery, but I didn't have the confidence for this at the time, and spent so much time fixing problems that I hardly had time to think of anything other than getting through each day.

I felt pushed to my physical and mental limits and there were times when I felt that if one more thing went wrong I wouldn't be able to cope. Of course that one more thing almost always did happen, and somehow we managed and got through it. I clearly remember walking into work as if through quicksand in total dread of the day ahead. The hardest part, however, was having to be on good form and uplifting when at work. I think that one of the most difficult elements of being the boss is that you're not allowed an 'off' day, and have to try and be an inspirational leader, even when you're feeling completely strung out and like hiding in a corner. After all, if you don't appear to believe in what you're doing, why on earth should those around you? I also have to admit that I was not always good at this. I'm not a screamer and shouter, but equally I'm not very good at hiding my emotions and my frustrations were often clearly to be seen when things went wrong. The problem in a sense was that I cared too much, and it DID matter if we had screwed up and let someone down.

The person I have to thank most of all for helping me get through this period is my wife Harriet. She didn't know it at the time, as I was very good at separating home from work and didn't want to burden her with my doubts and fears, but every night when I got home I was greeted by her happy smiling face and all the troubles of the day just fell away from me. She would be quickly followed by a whirlwind of tiny dressing gowns rushing to greet me, and the world was immediately a wonderful place. The greatest thing about all of the difficult times at work, when I was endlessly worried about the future and whether we would ever have enough money, was that we always had a lovely time at home and life was always fun despite living off a shoestring.

CHAPTER 4

Moving into Wholesale

By this time David had moved his office down to Cornwall and so we were now sending all purchase and sales invoices down to his office there on a weekly basis and they would send cheques back to me for signing and sending onto our suppliers. We still received quarterly accounts and these were generally completed towards the end of the month following the quarter. On one occasion I knew we had had good sales for the period and so was pretty optimistic that we must have made a reasonable profit. It was incredibly demoralising to be told we had only just made a tiny profit. It also made me realise how valuable it would be to have more up-to-date information.

We began to increase our wholesale business and it soon reached a point where it was becoming the majority of our business. The problem was that, while sales looked impressive and had reached over £600k, our profit wasn't, due to the much lower margins. We had to give away up to 40 per cent discount from our normal selling price to be competitive in this market, which naturally had a huge effect on our margins. If this model was to work, then we would badly need some serious volume.

Despite the extra space, we began to reach the limits of what we could handle on the basket and platter sales. Baskets had hit a buffer and were becoming more difficult to develop, not helped at all by the increased security measures thanks to the IRA risk. It is easy to forget what a threat the IRA was at this time and many of the cut-through roads in the City were blocked off, as well as there being vastly increased security in most offices, where our sellers would now need passes to enter the building.

Graham became keen to return to the world of picture framing and decided to set up his own company to do this. He had worked tirelessly and been an amazing help and a lot of fun to work with, and a big part of the company, but I could totally understand his decision. We had been struggling away just making ends meet for too long now, and it was hard to see much light at the end of the tunnel. I thought it was time to take stock and recognised it was time to make some big decisions. It was now early 1995 and the last few years had taken a lot out of all of us. We were lucky, in as much as we had survived when quite a few similar-sized companies had failed, but that wasn't enough and it was gruelling work, at least 10–14 hours every day, to go nowhere fast.

It was hard to see how we were going to develop the baskets or platter sales much further as they were both so difficult logistically, and were stretching us to our limit. Producing the sandwiches was the easy bit, and we could do a lot more of that, but not with the operational and delivery issues we were having to deal with on a daily basis. I discussed this with David, and we decided to take a massive gamble and stop selling platters and stop the basket rounds, and concentrate on the wholesale market. This meant giving up over 40 per cent of our business, and we were only just making a small profit anyway, but if we didn't clear the way and free ourselves up, it was hard to see any other way forward. We allowed three months for this transition and to let everyone we supplied have time to find an alternative supplier. We gave some of the basket rounds to a fledgling company that had just started, on the basis that they would pay us 10 per cent commission for the first six months. I thought this a fair deal, as rounds were hard to develop, but they never paid us a penny. It was an informal arrangement and it was more the principle that was disappointing, rather than the money, but my attitude is that as much as possible I will trust people, and if they let me down, then they will only do it once.

The main advantage of wholesale was that the orders were generally for a good size, and that deliveries could be made early the following morning, usually to a loading bay. No more rushing from pillar to post, parking on yellow lines and rushing upstairs to drop off 15 sandwiches for a meeting, or waiting on a street corner because a basket seller turned up late to start his round. This was a much simpler model. We would need volume though, and need it quite fast.

To explain a little about 'wholesale' business. In our world, this generally means selling to a contract caterer who in turn is providing the catering to large companies for their staff canteens (soon to be become known as staff restaurants – all very grand). Sandwich making might seem a simple task, but en masse it takes up a lot of room and is quite demanding. Apart from anything else, it is hard to know what your actual costs per sandwich are if your kitchen staff are making them up before getting on with the rest of their work. Then there is product development, quality control, quantity control, nutritional information, packaging, correct stocks of ingredients and so on. Of course it's easily possible for many kitchens, but there are many other things they would rather be doing. Very often over the years a company would try switching to making in-house and within a few months return to using us for these reasons.

We had taken the ground floor of Union Court, and a

small company, called Tuck Box, moved into the top floor a year or so later. The idea being that you could order a box of delicious food for picnics, events, or as a present. It was run by Danni Bain, and we occasionally sold them sandwiches to go in their boxes. As we worked a little more closely together I suggested that Danni might like to help us with sales when she had any spare time, particularly as some of the people she was approaching for corporate events might be potential clients for us. We did this on a commission basis, paying her a small retainer, so it was a very relaxed arrangement.

By 1995 the children were really beginning to grow up (seven, six and three years old) and the issue of schooling was becoming more and more important. They had been at the local church school two doors away when they were toddlers, and then we had managed to get them into a very nice school just off Sloane Square. The problem was that Stockwell was not the best place for good state schools, and we didn't know where they could go to next. Private school was completely out of the question, and it was quite hard to get into a state school outside one's own area. We were talking about this at a family gathering for my father's birthday one weekend, and discussing why the French system was so much better, and why couldn't/shouldn't we either live in France or at least have a similar system in this country. Two days later, my sister rang me and said that an old friend had rung her to say they were moving back from their house in France and to let her know if she knew anyone that might want to rent it – what a coincidence and what did I think? We hadn't discussed this with any intent at all – just the usual Sunday lunch moan and banter, but I was slightly intrigued and mentioned it to Harriet that night. Why not give her a ring? she suggested.

The thought of living abroad was very appealing: just the sense of being different and having a change in our lives, and who knows, if the right job opportunity came up, maybe we could end up living there, because we were only just scraping by as it was. The overriding influence, however, was the children's education, and if we could have a bit of adventure *and* have the children educated really well for free then it could be very tempting. We also thought that if we could get the children speaking fluent French, then we might be able to get them into the French Lycée which has schools in Clapham and South Kensington. They have a fantastic reputation and could provide a neat solution to our dilemma.

The friend was charming and said they had loved living there, but needed to move back. Their house was in Montelimar – known almost solely for its nougat, and most people drive past it on their way to Provence without even knowing it is there. They had a small son at the local school and so I asked her if she would mind speaking to the school and seeing if they might take three English children who didn't speak a word of French. She rang back the following day and said the school would be delighted to accept our children. 'Blimey, this could get serious,' I thought and rang Harriet and said, slightly tongue in cheek, 'We're moving to France.' 'Great,' she said with typical cheerfulness, 'when are we off?' We had had lunch on Sunday, I had spoken to my sister and her friend on Tuesday, and it was now Thursday. And the new school year started in four weeks . . .

Within that time we sold our car and bought a left-hand-drive car capable of towing a trailer, rented the house out through an agent for a year, and set off. We had agreed that we would try keeping Daily Bread going with me commuting every two weeks or so to France for a few days and see how things went. If we were lucky, we might love it there, and I might be able to get a job out there. I might not be able to find a great job in a provincial town in the middle of France, but at least the sun would shine a bit more. We rented a large trailer and packed everything we thought we'd need and set off for Dover. We had simply told the children that we were going to live in France and that it should be really good fun. Language was an issue as they literally didn't speak a word, but we reassured them that they would soon pick it up – hopefully taking more after their mother than their father. Luckily Harriet's French is excellent having lived in France for some of her misspent youth, and this was to prove essential as no one, including the head mistress of our huge new school, spoke a word of English.

We started early and drove all the way down to Montelimar, which is about 1½ hours south of Lyon. We arrived in darkness and couldn't for the life of us find the entrance to the house. It turned out that the house was on the edge of the town with a small side door onto the road into the town, while at the back was a huge garden with a separate drive that came off a completely different road from their address. We eventually found the drive and managed to get halfway up it before we couldn't get the trailer round the corner, and had to leave the car and trailer there for the night and walk the rest of the way to the house.

It was a lovely house and looked huge, but was in fact only one room deep. It's hard to believe now, but the following morning we walked to the school and dropped our three little angels off. It was of course a little difficult for them and a completely alien environment. Apart from anything else, the school used to be an army barracks and so was huge and austere-looking with a dusty parade ground in the middle and gigantic wooden doors to the main entrance. My most abiding memory, however, was of dropping off Ludo, our youngest, who was just three and clutching a small pillow that his class needed for their afternoon nap.

The following afternoon, when we had picked the children up from school, we reversed the car and trailer back down the drive and went up the steep and narrow road that ran by the side door of the house. We parked precariously with wooden blocks under the trailer wheels, and unpacked the whole thing as speedily as we could for fear of causing a traffic jam. The school and town centre were both within ten minutes' walk and so I drove the car and trailer back to England a few days later to drop off the trailer. I then drove out again after a week or so and used the train from then on.

I had taken a room in a neighbour's house in London and stayed there for a few months but soon decided to take up a friend's kind offer of staying in his house as he was often in the country and wasn't there. This made an enormous difference to my life, and I will always be incredibly grateful to him. I hadn't enjoyed staying with our neighbours at all as they were always arguing with each other, and I couldn't stand the atmosphere. To cap it all the friend with the house even refused to accept any rent and just asked that I paid the cleaner once a week. Even this made a difference as every penny counted at this time, and the small rent I had agreed to pay our neighbours was a useful saving.

The children settled into their new life pretty quickly and I established a rough routine of being in London for ten days and then France for five. The advantage was that I could work very hard in London, and not feel I had to get back to help with the children etc. in the evening, and then spend five lovely days with the family. Harriet was truly incredible throughout the whole adventure and coped amazingly well, living by herself in a large house, looking after three small children, having to pick them up every lunch time, drop them back in the afternoon, and *then* do homework with them in the evening – and all in a foreign language. I really admired what she was doing and was continually astounded by her resilience and cheerful disposition. The children were also amazing throughout our time in France and adapted well to their new environment. It was never easy saying goodbye, but we just had to look forward to the next time.

The unexpected consequence of the whole escapade was that we all became much closer as a family. We'd always been a very tight-knit unit, but this experience really showed us what fun we could have just as a family by ourselves. In England we would almost always be doing things with other families at weekends or holidays and now that wasn't possible. Instead, we would drive off to the mountains or to a river with a picnic and spend the day making dams or playing in the natural pools created by the rivers. In the winter we would drive for two hours up into the local mountains and ski in a lovely tiny resort that had about three lifts and even provided a heated hut where you could warm your soup and eat a picnic. Courcheval it wasn't, but what a wonderful way to teach the children such a great sport, and the most expensive part of the whole day was the petrol to get there.

Daily Bread had started supplying Harvey Nichols with sandwiches and that was great, mainly for the profile it gave us as the numbers weren't huge, and it was a good name to drop to potential clients. We had also started to supply London Zoo in Regents Park which then led onto supplying the Natural History Museum as it was run by the same catering company. This was a wonderful contract as we were always busy with one of them, and particularly during school holidays and half terms. If it was sunny then the zoo was frantic and if it rained everyone went to the museum and so we could shift sandwiches from one to the other as necessary. We had about four vans by this time and they were all refrigerated. It is incredible, again, how much has changed in the years since we started. For the first four years or so we had no refrigerated vans and never had any complaints or illnesses (and we saw the same customers every day then, so would have known) and nowadays every delivery must be below 8°C and if a van is temperature probed at 8.1° the entire delivery will most likely be rejected. I am almost obsessed with hygiene and we have always been ruthless in maintaining really high standards in the kitchen, but I do think the Health and Safety lot have become far too powerful and self-serving and, the way things are going, people will start dying from the common cold in a few years' time as it'll be the first thing they have come across that hasn't been zapped of any conceivable bacteria.

Anyway, back to vans. The trouble with vans is that they need drivers, and if there's a more unreliable category of employee, then I have yet to come across it. We had endless problems and never knew who would or wouldn't turn up for work. As a result we were horribly compromised and often put up with behaviour that we would never tolerate now. Even if they were 45 minutes late for work, and the whole delivery round would be delayed, it was still better than having no driver at all – and it took at least three days to properly train a new driver to do the round. Of course, the spare driver was still myself and every day I would be making a delivery of some sort, and often for the whole morning, with the phone regularly ringing at 5am to tell me I was on 'driver duty' that day. By this time Kamel, who had joined us three years previously working in the kitchen, volunteered to take care of our deliveries as he knew London pretty well and reckoned he could do it. It was an unusual progression for a kitchen manager, but I knew he was dedicated and his heart was in the right place, and nothing could be worse than carrying on as we were. He slowly got to grips with it, and in his own style developed a way of running the transport department that would see us right for the next 15 years. He is by nature not good at communicating, and this would often create friction between us. I came to realise that trying to manage him was like trying to herd cats, and so pretty much gave up. As long as the job was done, that was fine by me, and to be fair to him, it was a very demanding 24/7 role as there was very often something wrong with either a van or a driver and he would have to deal with it. Because of the London Zoo and Natural History Museum we were now also operating seven days a week. I have always appreciated how much weight he took off my shoulders by taking care of this side of the business.

We had quite a few small wholesale clients now, and I had even tried Buckingham Palace, but they were happy using a local sandwich shop if they ever needed sandwiches, but we still didn't supply any of the big caterers. I tried endlessly to arrange meetings to sell to them and every time they would say how good our sandwiches were, and then ask for the price and that would be that. The only way they were going to ever use us at this time was if we were cheaper than their current supplier, and they were buying at what I thought were ridiculous prices, and certainly not possible for us to match. It again became more and more clear that we would need good volume to take advantage of the benefits of scale – after all, making 1050 instead of 1000 tuna sandwiches is incredibly easy and cost effective compared with just making 50. I was also determined to stick to offering premium sandwiches and be known for that. Price would therefore never be our trump card, and instead offering great quality and a great service would be our selling points. The big problem was that this isn't what the big contract caterers wanted at this point. The cheaper they could buy, the greater the margin they could make, and that was their driver, and what unit managers would be judged on. As long as their clients were more or less happy, then that would do.

By mid-1996 Harriet and I had agreed that we would give it one more year in France and we rented our house in Stockwell for another year. Montelimar itself was a lovely town and the surrounding countryside was stunning, and we loved feeling we were living a slightly different life. The children had also settled in pretty well to their new school. There was certainly little chance of me getting a job there, and every single person we spoke to advised against even thinking of setting up my own business, if for no better reason than their national insurance tax for employees was so high that trying to run a small business legitimately was almost impossible. We had agreed to rent the house up until June, when the school broke up, for a very reasonable rate, which enabled the owners to charge a fortune for the July and August holiday months. The rent we received for our house in Stockwell paid for my travel and the rent on the French house. So we didn't save any money, but we had had a great time, the children now all spoke French, and of course the main point had been getting a really good free education, and that had gone brilliantly. We returned to spend the summer in England camping with our parents and visiting friends. This was fun, but ultimately very tiring and it was with some relief that we returned to France in September. The plan was to get the children properly bilingual which would take another year, and then we could all return and hopefully get them into the Lycée in London.

CHAPTER 5

Tough Going

Meanwhile, back in Blighty, things were getting tricky.

It had been fun working a little with Danni, but she couldn't devote too much time to our cause. An idea she did come up with, however, was developing a vegetarian range that would, in contrast to most vegetarian offerings at that time, taste really good and make no effort to be too low calorie or appeal to weight watchers. They would be naughty but nice. We called them Wicked Wedges and had a logo designed with a devil and separate labels made. The idea was that this would give us another angle to hit potential clients with and Seham came up with some amazing recipes, one of which – goats' cheese, roasted pine nuts, asparagus and sun dried tomatoes on tomato bread – became our (hate the word) 'signature' sandwich and has remained on our menu ever since. It wasn't cheap, and it certainly wasn't for the weight conscious, but it would end up selling very well. The trouble is that it didn't sell any at the time. We couldn't shift this great new idea for love or money.

Seham had been an amazing support throughout our time in France and would always shoo me off to the station insisting that I wasn't to worry about anything and that everything would be fine. I had got my travel down to a fine art by now and always left work at the last possible moment, generally having to run down the platform to catch the Eurostar. I normally went via Lille and the journey took about eight hours, a lot of which I would spend working on my laptop. I was spending all my time thinking about work, and I had a lot to think about. We had recently lost some business when a caterer decided to switch to another supplier because they were cheaper and we were, for the first time since we had started, losing money. I was by now getting monthly management accounts which was good, but the reading of them was not good at all. As David had always pointed out, and it is a truism I often still quote, you can break even forever, but only lose money for a very finite period of time.

We badly needed more sales. By July 1996 we had turned over £850K and made a small profit. I now knew our model could work, but we had to get some volume going through the kitchen. Danni was by now concentrating on her own business and I placed an advert in *The Times* for a salesman. I had literally one reply. Gill Murphy had responded out of idle curiosity as she had built up and sold her own sandwich company a few years previously. We immediately got on well and she said she'd give it a go, but had young children and so would need to work around them. We agreed a 'commission only' deal which would give her all the flexibility she needed, and of course it didn't cost me anything if she didn't produce any sales. I just wish we had maintained this structure with most of our future salesmen – it would have saved us a fortune . . .

One day I was queuing to pay in WH Smith and I picked up a book by Anthony Robbins, a well-known 'life coach'. I'm as cynical as the next man about most American mumbo-jumbo self-help stuff, but a quick flick through this book intrigued me, and on any page I turned to there seemed to be some good common sense. I bought it and was immediately fascinated by it. There were two big things in its favour: I had a lot of time to read while I was travelling and I was by myself in London. And I was ready for any help I could get. I had been struggling with the business for a few years now and was finding it harder and harder to be upbeat and motivate myself. I knew the business could make sense and be profitable if we could get some more sales, but began to doubt myself, and wondered if I wasn't just fooling myself. In the book, called *Awaken the Giant Within* (clearly a book *not* to be judged by its cover) there are many anecdotes of people feeling a similar way, and what they did to change things, and I found this really inspiring. The basis of the book is that we are born with the most incredible computer, but not given any manual on how to use it, and that there *are* ways of changing how one thinks. I was spending a lot of time despairing at my situation, struggling to see any light at the end of the tunnel and feeling pretty low and lacking in energy. The main lesson I took from the book was to pick up on when I was having a negative thought, try and visualise the thought, and then, as if pulling the aerial out of the back of the TV, replace the image with a fuzzy screen. And then force myself to think of something, anything, positive. It could be what's for dinner that evening, a film to see, holiday to look forward to, anything positive. The immediate benefit for me was incredible and I would use this trick almost every day while I was shaving and thinking about the day ahead and all the things I was worried about, with the result that I would go into work feeling much more perky and energetic, which was not only uplifting for those around me, but put me in a much better position to deal with the issues that had been bothering me in the first place. Without realising it, I had developed a habit over the past few years of dwelling on all the things that worried me at work, and it was a pattern I had to break. After all, as I was to learn later, if I kept doing and thinking the same things, why should the result ever be any different?

Seeing the almost immediate benefit I had got out of this book, I became really interested in learning. I went for a meeting with a life coach which didn't come to anything, but during our conversation he mentioned that he had just been on a sailing holiday and that he had been told that a possible cure for seasickness was to look at the horizon. I was driving back from the meeting when I reflected on this and it struck me that it was also a great life lesson. The next day I printed out and stuck on the top of my laptop a small note: 'To avoid seasickness, look to the horizon.' Again, this was to try and break the habit of navel gazing and to remind myself to look up and forward. One of the things you are taught as a motorbike rider is to always look at where you want to go, not at a hazard. If you are looking at the tree you want to avoid, the chances are you'll hit it – same lesson.

Another book that had quite an influence on me at this time was completely different and is easily the best book I have ever read. *The Fountainhead* by Ayn Rand. Rand explains her philosophy through the characters in a novel and it's based on two architects, one is a preppy and does all the right things, and the other is a rebel who will only design what he believes is good, rather than what he is told is good. Their paths, and fortunes, cross as the book progresses. It is brilliantly written and the central message is the importance of being responsible for your own actions and living life on your terms, not those that maybe foisted upon you. She also brilliantly describes what she refers to as 'second-handers'. These are people who make decisions in their life not for themselves, so much as for what others will think of them, and thereby live a 'second-hand' existence. We all know the type. I loved this book, and it somehow gave me a little confidence and reassurance to continue along my own path.

One of the benefits of having Gill around was that I had to be positive around her, to encourage her that we really were good and that everything was looking pretty rosy. This was not easy when I had a sick feeling in the bottom of my stomach for much of the time – the books weren't *that* good – and I had to keep this up to the rest of the staff as well for the same reason. It was so hard getting business that I hatched a new plan. What about opening our own shop if it could be done cheaply enough, and that way we would be our own client? And if one worked, then we could open lots of them. A friend ran a department store in Brixton and I agreed with him that we would take a small corner of their ground floor. We called this Sandwich Express and spent about £10,000 converting the space. This was almost the last roll of the dice and was done as much out of desperation as anything else, but it had to work.

It didn't.

Try as we might, and we opened early and closed late, handed out flyers, offered special deals, did everything we could think of to shift sandwiches, it was to no avail. We needed to sell about 200 sandwiches a day to break even, and we sold about 30. Yes, Brixton wasn't the best choice to try selling premium sandwiches, but it was the only place I could think of where we could experiment without it costing a fortune, although £10k was a lot of money to us. Driving from our unit in Union Court to the shop, which I did most days, were the most depressing journeys I've ever had and, bugger all the positive stuff, I felt absolutely bloody terrible. Luckily we were able to pull out after three months, which was a great relief. If there was one big lesson I learnt from my commodity days, it was never to chase a loss. If something goes wrong, get out and live to fight another day. I saw countless clients hold onto loss-making positions in the hope the market would turn . . . and end up losing a fortune.

There are however exceptions to this rule, as will become clear. So, now things were looking really dire. The shop had eaten into our cash reserves, we were losing £2k a week and we had a total of £40k retained profit in the company – the total result of ten years of backbreaking work. I stopped drawing a salary at this point and would have to live off the tiny savings I had put aside. I never told anyone at work this, as I didn't want to alarm them, but the writing was on the wall and our days were numbered. At what point would I pull the plug? While we still had a little cash left in the business, or run it to its natural conclusion? I discussed this with David and Harriet. It was now October 1996 and we agreed that we would close the business at the end of the year if things hadn't picked up. Confidence at this point was not great. I hadn't minded not making a fortune in the City because I hadn't worked that hard and wasn't particularly interested in the work, and there was always the thought that, if I had pulled my finger out, I could have done alright. But not to make any money when you've really worked hard and thrown everything at it, that's quite another thing. I felt stupid for having carried on for so long and, worst of all, I felt that I had let my family down. How was I going to support them? Yes, we could sell the house and free up some cash there, but selling the family home was a pretty depressing thought, and we'd still need to live somewhere and I would still need to bring in some cash to live off and who would employ a forty-one-year-old that had underachieved in the City and then failed at running his own business? I saw quite a bit of Graham and my sister during this time and they were great at looking after me when I was in London. Graham's business had gone well, and I remember feeling so glad they weren't also still relying on Daily Bread for their daily bread.

In November I had started to look around at what else I could possibly do and responded to an advertisement in the *Sunday Times* placed by a company that was looking for chief executives to join their consultancy business. I felt I'd learnt quite a lot and had at least built up a company that turned over £800k from scratch, and that should be worth something, even if it wasn't making any money. I went for an interview in Pall Mall and met the owner. From his red braces stretching across his over-lunched stomach, to his smug jowly face, I disliked him immediately and I sat there filling in a psychometric assessment form thinking to myself, has it really come to this? The deal turned out to be that I would pay him £10k which would give me some training in their consultancy method and I would then go and get clients to consult and we would split the income 50/50. Thanks, but no thanks. God, I wished that Daily Bread could work, because from this initial glimpse, I didn't like the view from the other side one bit.

Amidst all this despair, I read an interesting booklet called 'Have your best year yet' or something like that. The idea was to write down what you had achieved in the past six months, and then write what you'd like to achieve in the next six months, one year and five years. Part of the idea of writing down what you had achieved is that it is important to occasionally pause and reflect on what you have done. 'Not much,' I thought to myself as I started to fill in the booklet, and then I began to realise that we had actually done quite a lot, not least of which was developing the Wicked Wedges idea and taking on Gill. Gill had been a great asset since she started with us a few months before, and had already introduced some new business, although obviously not as much as we needed at that point. I remember being a little inspired by this exercise and it provided a brief, welcome, relief from the feeling of desperation I felt most of the time.

Harriet had been fantastic throughout the tribulations at Daily Bread and we had one memorable chat about life when we arrived for some reason at the station in France a couple of hours before my train was due to leave. We went to a local café and had a real 'so what are we going to do with our lives' conversation. We agreed that if the company closed we would have to down-scale, and maybe we should try living in a small cottage in Cornwall and I could get by doing some basic job or other. By this stage Harriet was getting more and more excited, to the point where it was actually beginning to sound like it would be quite fun. This wasn't put on for my benefit, she really meant it, and by the time my train arrived I was feeling really quite upbeat for the first time in months. Life would go on and we would be fine. What a brilliant person to be married to.

Christmas quickly came and went and the next thing I knew it was mid-January and we were still limping on. So much for my discipline of cutting my losses. Gill had a few leads for potential new business, and we had slowed our losses a little by cutting back on everything possible, but it was still looking pretty grim and I think I had by this stage resigned myself to seeing what would be. I just didn't have the heart to pull the plug on a business in which everyone had worked so hard. It was too awful to contemplate when it actually came to it, and I didn't have the bottle.

By mid-February we had about six weeks to go before we ran out of cash. The big caterers were still not interested in us and when I rang them they would ask me to put a price list in the post and that would be that. We were trying every big company we could think of and speaking directly to their catering departments, trying to drum up business, and one day I spoke to the catering manager at one of the KPMG sites in London. I went to see him with samples of the Daily Bread and Wicked Wedge ranges. He looked at the Wicked Wedge samples and said that he might be interested in trying some of them during a healthy eating promotion he was planning in a couple of weeks. I naturally didn't discuss their calorific values – they were vegetarian, and that was quite healthy enough for anyone.

KPMG used two other sandwich suppliers at this time and so we sold about twenty sandwiches a day during the promotion. The manager said they had sold really well and he liked what we had done, and I suggested he might like to see if our Daily Bread range would also go down well with his customers. He didn't have much to lose, and if his customers didn't like them, or weren't prepared to pay a little more for them, then they would vote with their feet and we wouldn't trouble him any more. He already had two suppliers, but wasn't that happy with one of them, and decided to give us a go on a trial basis.

And on such things does the fate of a business sometimes hinge. Within three months we were their sole supplier and, better still, he turned out to be the area manager for the other five KPMG sites in London and we were soon supplying all of them. His company also catered for masses of other businesses in London, and so we now had a huge new potential avenue for business. We had turned the corner and escaped by the skin of our teeth. Many years later I took the manager out for lunch (he was by now covering the whole of London) and told him the story. He, of course, had no idea, but it was nice to thank him and tell him how much I owed to him.

By the end of July we had recovered our losses, turned over

£1m and actually made a small profit for the year – something unthinkable only a few months before. This was incredibly exciting, but now we must make sure that we not only kept the business we had gained, but also found some new clients. I wanted to run as far and as fast as I could away from the position we had been in and would throw everything I had at achieving this.

CHAPTER 6

On the Up

By this stage we were still under the radar of most of our competitors, being quite small and having entered the whole-sale world only comparatively recently. I was very happy to keep it this way, and I also felt we were on quite a different path from the rest of them. It seemed to me that every other sandwich manufacturer had a very similar offer. The sand-wiches were OK, but not particularly nice, and keeping prices down and selling as cheaply as they needed to get new business seemed to be the common criteria. This was fair enough, as that was what most caterers demanded at the time. I wanted to be a niche player, offering a premium product at a higher price for those that wanted it. This would mean using better quality ingredients and more filling to make really good versions of the most popular varieties, as well as pushing the boundaries to produce more exotic recipes using unusual hand-crafted breads. I knew this wasn't for everyone, but could imagine the likes of the Opera House or some of the large City companies wanted something better than they were currently getting. We could even perhaps sit alongside some of our competitors on the shelves, certainly in the larger companies where there would naturally be a diverse customer base. I knew this would limit our size, but I would rather that than become another large, faceless, industrial company.

Gill Murphy had really got into her stride by this point and was bringing in some great business including the BBC and they were to be one of our biggest clients for the next few years. It was essential we offered an outstanding service to ensure we kept the business, and also to keep Gill happy. She was paid 5 per cent of all sales she generated for a year from a new client starting and so, if we screwed up and lost one of her clients, she could be pretty badly out of pocket. And pretty badly pissed off (she was never shy of letting us know this), and a pissed-off saleswoman was the last thing we needed just as we were getting some traction. As it turned out, thanks to Seham and Kamel doing an increasingly outstanding job, we kept almost all our business and Gill was soon earning more than me (I had, by the way, started paying myself again – it wasn't *that* easy . . .). And that was absolutely fine by me; the more she earned that happier I was.

As we developed more business, things improved dramatically, although the predominant emotion was a sense of relief and there remained a lingering uncertainty as to how long it would all last. Our recent struggles did however have some interesting influences on how I ran the company. I normally try to be as open and straightforward as I can with everyone, but the past few years had been very strenuous and I felt I could never let my true concerns about the future of the company show, for fear of ruining morale. I had also not told any of the staff how close to the edge we had been, not paying myself and so on, for the same reason. I'm not saying this is right or wrong – nowadays I think I would be a lot more frank – but it's just how it was and what I thought was for the best at the time. As a result, when things started going a bit better, big figures in our management accounts such as turnover, ingredient costs, distribution, packaging and direct labour were always shared with everyone, but I continued to keep our operating profit/loss to myself and David. This was a habit I continued for the rest of the time I ran the business. One of the great advantages it gave me a few years later, when things were going very well, but we had had a poor month on say ingredient costs (always measured as a percentage of turnover) was that I could jump up and down a bit and say we must improve this area, without anyone saying, 'What are you complaining about, we've made a good profit this month anyway.' Besides, if it ain't broke, don't fix it, and we all seemed perfectly happy. I had always said that I would take care of people and pay them better when we could afford it, and few things have given me more pleasure than rewarding that trust as the years went on.

It was now mid-1997 and we had returned from our French sojourn. We had decided to sell our house in Stockwell and to buy a small flat with a view to hopefully buying somewhere in the country eventually, as we could get a lot more for our money. We needed the London base for my work and the children's school. Part of the thinking behind this was also that we wanted to feel we were moving forward, rather than simply returning to the same house and carrying on as before. I had some concern how we might cope with our new life, as we had become quite used to our routine over the past couple of years, and it had gone so well, but it all slotted into place very easily, and nothing could beat having the family back again. We couldn't have done it for any longer, as we missed not being all together too much, but to this day we all look back on it as the best thing we have done, and a brilliant adventure. It is an irony that we would never have done it if wasn't for the fact that we didn't have any money. We bought a very small two-bedroom flat in Clapham, put 90 per cent of our stuff into storage and lived hugger-mugger for the next 18 months – what a contrast, but it seemed perfectly normal. It's incredible how much clobber we accumulate in life, and how much of it one is totally happy living without. Sasha had gone into the Lycée in Clapham as planned, Ludo to a small French feeder school for the Lycée and for the eldest, Jimbo, we had taken the giant step of taking up a place at a private fee-paying prep school. He had found it hardest to adapt to the French school, but it was mainly his endless energy that needed an outlet, and it was a gamble we felt worth taking. It proved an immediate success and was one of the best decisions we ever made. We reconciled ourselves to the fact that we would do everything we could to fund his way through the private system, and the other two should be fine at the Lycée.

We were getting more and more busy at Daily Bread and taking on a lot more work, and it was as if we had suddenly reached the crest of a long steep hill and were at last on a downhill section. To cap it all, out of the blue Buckingham Palace rang me and asked if I would go and see them. The reason I've never been a great salesman is that I hate hassling people and so I had characteristically not rung them since my initial call a couple of years previously. It turned out they needed sandwiches for their extra staff when they opened the State rooms in the Palace to the public in August and September, and were a little concerned that the hygiene standards at the local shop they had been using might not be up to standard. We started supplying them that summer. What a perfect client for us to have, and the effect on morale was fantastic. My constant mantra at work had for some time been that we must be the best. The best quality, and the best service, otherwise why would anyone use us? We weren't the cheapest and we didn't offer national distribution, and we didn't have the biggest product range either, so we *had* to be the best. And now we were supplying the most prestigious institution in the country. For the first two years of supplying them it was quite a complicated operation as we had to put individual names on each sandwich as they were ordered specifically. After that the Palace luckily changed the system and simply ordered the total needed for each day and their staff took them on a first come, first served basis.

The rest of the year rushed by and we were determined to keep things moving and not to let go of this break we had been given. We were paying David's company 3 per cent of turnover to do all the accounting work for us which was fine, and meant the more business we did, the more they were paid, but it was becoming increasingly ridiculous sending a huge envelope down to Cornwall every week where the purchase and sales invoices would be recorded and then filed. Inevitably sometimes an invoice wouldn't be put in the envelope and we would have to make subsequent adjustments. It seemed to me that we would benefit hugely from having all the accounts done 'in-house'. To have someone on site who could pop down at any time to 'goods-in' to check on a purchase invoice they didn't understand, or talk to the admin team about any sales issues, must make sense. David and I had not been so close for the last couple of years, and I wouldn't blame him at all if he hadn't had enough sometimes of this struggling company he was involved with in London. He had been invaluable at the beginning and also through many of the developing years, always a sound head to consult/shoulder to cry on, and encouraging when things were tough. He was also quite a dominant personality and his way was the right way . . . full stop.

He came down to London and, while I'd mentioned moving the accounting function in-house before, thought the time had come to properly address it. He could be quite forceful, and when I brought the subject up he went into a rant that turned into a tirade about how complicated their role was and did I know they did daily cashbook reconciliations and lots of other accounting jargon I didn't understand. The company wouldn't run without his accounting team and if he wasn't to do it, who would and did I have ANY idea how much more that would cost?? We'd had similar, less explosive discussions before, but this time I'd had enough and, for the first and I think only time in my life, I lost my temper. Slamming my fist down on the table I said, 'How dare you talk to me like that? If I can't bring up a perfectly reasonable subject without you throwing your toys out of the pram then I'm not prepared to carry on as we are.' He was quite shocked by this as no one ever spoke to him in such terms (later on the admin staff told me they were really quite worried as they'd never heard such a noise coming out of my office). We then quietened down and worked out how we should proceed, if this was the path I had set myself on. An obvious issue was his shareholding and I said I would be very happy for him to keep his shares as I was really grateful for everything he had done for the company and me. To his credit he said that he'd like me to buy his shares off him as, if the company got into trouble they would become worthless and he'd find that irritating, and if it went on to do great things then I would find it irritating paying him when he hadn't been involved during those years. He certainly leant in the direction of the first option and so I agreed with him and he left it to me to come up with a valuation.

Valuing a minority shareholding in a small private company is far from a scientific matter and I talked to as many people as I could about this. Inevitably some suggested playing hard ball and paying a nominal sum, while others came up with various different multiples based on the past year's figures, or the average of the last two year's or three year's figures. Of course, the last three years looked pretty terrible, while the last year (we were three-quarters of the way through our 1997/98 year at the time) looked much better. There was no easy answer and I came to realise it was as much a moral issue as a straight financial calculation. I finally settled on a figure at the top of any of the calculations, which David happily accepted. We had been too good friends for too long, and he had been an amazing help and I would much rather overpay a bit than have him thinking I had paid the minimum I could get away with. I remember being quite nervous as, maybe he was right, I didn't have a clue what was involved as far as accounting was concerned and maybe it was much more complicated than I realised, and what if we DID screw up?

We agreed to carry on as we were for a few more months while I found someone to take over the accounting function. I didn't know where to look, and so used Reed Recruitment initially. They came up with a guy who seemed to have the necessary qualifications and said he was experienced in a similar role. He was a complete disaster. My God, maybe David was right after all . . .

It took a few months for it to become clear how unsuited he was as he could do the basics, but he was quite a creepy character, and every single time I left or arrived at the unit throughout the day I would find him outside smoking which drove me mad after a while. He then had the nerve to say he didn't have enough time to do some of his work. The cheek of it. A friend put me in touch with an accountancy company in Croydon. They offered to be our auditors and said they had a bright young recently qualified chartered accountant leaving them, as he wanted to work in a small business rather than for an accountancy firm.

Things were at last slotting into place and James Knight-Adams joined us at the end of 1998 as our accountant. He immediately got to grips with the whole accountancy function and set up systems that we continued to use from then on. He was fizzing with ideas and became an invaluable member of the team, being happy to roll his sleeves up and help the admin dept out, make an extra delivery in emergencies, or whatever it took. He was also the most computer literate of all of us, and so took care of our basic computer issues. We were never going to be a company where everyone had their set roles and didn't stray from them, because there was always a flurry of activity and we would sometimes need all hands on deck. There was also no job I hadn't done in the business (apart from the accountancy function), and there should be no job anyone else wasn't prepared to do. If the drains got blocked, whoever was around would deal with it and that's how it had to be. We had as little hierarchy as possible. As far as we were concerned, everyone had an equally important role and should therefore be treated with equal respect, and no one should ever think they were above anyone else or not be prepared to help them out. They may have different jobs, and they may be paid more, but that didn't mean that they were better.

By this stage we had moved production to the day before, with an order cut-off time of 2.30pm the day prior to delivery. This was how every other sandwich manufacturer was operating, which didn't necessarily make it a good thing, but the reality was that we simply couldn't cope with making sandwiches during the night and then having an increasingly complex allocation process before loading onto the vans and being delivered. It was all far too tight and cracks were beginning to show. So here is a brief explanation of how we now worked, which was to remain pretty much unchanged from this point on.

The kitchens started at 8.00am and would make up 80 per

cent of the anticipated orders for that day during the morning. This would naturally vary according to the day of the week.

Clients would telephone their orders into our admin dept up until 2.30pm, and if they hadn't placed an order we would ring them. We had by this stage ditched our old spreadsheets and bought a system designed for the sandwich industry, and the admin dept would enter the orders onto this, then print production sheets by 3pm showing the total amounts of each variety to be made for the day. Seham would then deduct the sandwiches we had already made in the morning from the totals needed and make up the balance, finishing by about 6pm. The admin dept then printed out all the delivery notes and labels and give them to the allocators.

The allocators picked the sandwiches ordered by each client first, and then applied that client's labels by hand. Each client could have their own prices on their labels, which was a fantastic service but made this part of the operation very cumbersome. The allocators would then divide the completed orders, along with delivery notes, into delivery rounds. The drivers would come in between 4am and 6am, pick up their round and hope to have finished dropping the sandwiches off by around 11.00am. Interrupting all this were pretty constant emergency deliveries, often helping a client out (good emergency), or making up for us making a mistake (bad emergency).

Invoices would be sent out each Monday for the previous week's deliveries and James acted as credit controller, amongst every other financial role at this time, and would be responsible for getting the money in.

Each day was quite a logistical challenge and endlessly interrupted by day-to-day problems. Typical issues we would have to deal with were pretty much as they always had been, starting with late deliveries – everyone wanted their delivery at pretty much the same time, ie before 9am, so this remained a constant headache – or deliveries would be short, or delivered to the wrong place. And this assumed the admin dept had processed the correct order in the first place and the computers and printers had worked without a hitch. We very rarely had quality complaints, and if we did, jumped onto it immediately and made any changes we needed to. Our whole sales pitch was that we offered a premium service, and we had to live by this every day as we were only as good as that day's delivery. We had taken on an admin manager, Maggie, to help us get organised and she did a great job. She improved the whole department and insisted we bought new printers instead of having to spend hours every week repairing the old ones and trying to un-stick the labels that had come off and stuck to the rollers.

Sales began to really take off at this point and there was a real buzz about the place. It was amazingly exciting, and we had to run as fast as we could to keep up with everything. One of the great advantages of supplying KPMG was that our reputation was spreading and our name was getting round to other unit managers within the same contract catering group. We started getting calls from them asking us to go and see them and this made a wonderful contrast to years of being ignored.

There was something else going on at this time and this is where we were most lucky. The business world was changing, and more and more people were beginning to stop eating out and instead stayed at their desks for lunch. Pret à Manger were really getting going by now and raising the standards on the High Street. Increasingly, contract caterers were getting used to the sight of their customers going out at lunch time and returning shortly with a Pret sandwich. If they were going to stop losing so much custom, and being given a hard time about the quality of the sandwiches on their shelves, they would have to improve their offer. We were always there to help out, of course, and we were the only producer that came close to their quality at the time, having always concentrated on the premium market. We were suddenly in the pound seats, and our turnover doubled to over £2m by July 1999. Whenever asked if I regarded Pret as a competitor, my answer has always been the opposite. They have been nothing but a good thing and helped raise standards more than any other company. Their operation is very complicated and it will have taken incredible management to achieve what they have done. From good-quality consistent sandwiches through to having happy helpful staff, they're a class act and deserve every bit of success they've had. Our sandwiches were sometimes not as good as theirs as that would have made us too uncompetitive in the wholesale world, but we were a lot better than any of our competitors and we had to make sure we kept it that way.

Things were going so well, and yet old habits die hard, and we were still operating in a very hand-to-mouth way. I thought it was time to try and professionalise ourselves – constant improvement, onwards and upwards, and all that sort of thing – and decided to employ an ex-production manager from the New Covent Garden Soup Company. Seham had been doing an amazing job, but we both assumed we could learn a lot from a real pro and that the kitchen would be transformed into a slick trouble-free temple of production in no time. After all, if we could get to this point in our own untrained, ramshackle way, imagine what a pro could help us achieve? It sadly didn't work, mainly because we were in the habit of working at a much faster pace than he was used to, and a few months later we continued in our own ramshackle ways without him.

I was working flat out at this time, and saw that Anthony Robbins was holding a two-day seminar down in Cardiff over a weekend. I thought I'd go and see what I could learn as I'd found his book so helpful. It cost about £500 which was a lot of money, but I thought I'd learnt so much already, and that I would 'invest in myself' to see if I could get any further benefit from him. I arrived on Friday night to be greeted by the sound of 2000 devotees clapping along to a loud soundtrack. What made them do it I've no idea, and then when the main man himself arrived it was as if a pop star had just arrived on stage. He revved everyone up in the hall, and then we went outside to do a mass fire-walk. There were about twenty lines of people all queuing in front of beds of hot coals. The idea, we had been told, is that anything is possible if you are mentally prepared and it was all about mind over matter. Everyone was chanting 'cool waters' or something similar with their hands waving in the air while they waited. I couldn't stand it and stood there silently thinking, 'What the hell am I doing on a Friday night *here*?' When I got to the front a young supervisor looked at me inquisitively and asked in a slightly patronising manner if I was OK and ready. I said I was ready, just couldn't do all this chanting business. 'Well, it's very important to do it while you walk over the coals,' she said. I walked silently over the coals, wondering all the time why they weren't burning me.

I went along the next morning, thinking it might have all calmed down a bit and I might learn something, but not a bit of it. The lunatics were off again, the soundtrack booming away once more, and when Robbins came on and urged us all to love each other and give each other a hug it was the final straw. A supervisor came over and asked if I was OK, to which I said I was fine, I was just worried about everyone else. I left after ten minutes. I had a Honda Blackbird 1100cc bike at the time and must have made the record time for the journey from Cardiff to the Isle of Wight where the family were staying with friends. The book was brilliant, but the live version couldn't have been more awful. I determined to continue to enjoy and use the good stuff I'd read, and to eradicate the Cardiff experience from my mind. It had been one of those instances which was actually quite funny, but it wasn't £500 worth of funny, and that was irritating.

We were always looking to improve everything that we did, and because we were making it up as we went along, there often lurked an insecurity that questioned whether we were doing the right thing or not. The important thing, though, was to keep learning and I loved listening to anyone that might offer advice, or reading business books that I thought might be relevant to us. I love the saying that we have one mouth and two ears and that they should be used in that proportion, and I think this is never truer than in business. Our main competitor at this stage was a company called Breadwinner and they took it too far, I felt, when they had their new kitchens and offices emblazoned with Japanese motivational words such as Kaizan, or something similar – I think it means continual improvement. Ridiculous idea, but very fashionable at the time, and I love the idea of the average kitchen worker looking up at these huge strange words and thinking, 'What the hell's that all about . . . ?'

Thinking of competitors, I never had a desire to become part of the sandwich-making world at large, and we never really communicated with our competitors. This stemmed from my drive to build a business, rather than a sandwich business. Our business happened to be sandwiches, and we would have to make sure they were the best sandwiches, but it was not through any gastronomically motivated desire to improve the eating habits of the great British public that pushed me on. There was a British Sandwich Association which produced a quarterly magazine that seemed to give its members an opportunity to pat themselves on the back, but I've never been very clubbable and didn't join it. I was also a little nervous of become friendly with people that we might be trying to take business away from, and didn't want my hands tied. I also didn't have time to go off to meetings and gatherings and wanted to keep my head down and simply concentrate on the job in hand. We were still quite small fry as a sandwich producer and so being below the radar and maintaining a low profile suited us fine.

CHAPTER 7

Growing Pains

By 1999 James said he could really do with some help on accounts and would also like to get more involved in helping improve other aspects of the business. One of the issues we had to deal with was that while it was great dealing with contract caterers, the drawback was that they demanded anything up to 90 days credit. This meant that the more business we did with them the more our cash was stretched as we had to pay our staff and suppliers at the end of every month. Cashflow was therefore critical and would have to be managed extremely carefully if we were going to be able to fund our growth. (It's a weird aspect of growing a business, that you actually need money to fund the growth, but is the reality for many companies. Companies don't necessarily go bust because they are running at a loss, they go bust because they run out of cash.) We advertised for an accounts assistant and must have been pretty desperate, because we interviewed a chap called Terry Ryder and took him on. Terry had arrived for the interview with his tie half undone and then proceeded to immediately complain about the traffic on his journey to us. The last thing I needed was someone who can be this negative at an interview I thought, 'I want bright and sparky people around me.' But we did take him on as he had the best experience of the candidates we interviewed and, in-credibly, over the next few years he became a complete superstar and a totally invaluable member of the team.

Perhaps I should have learnt from this experience, because I dread to think of the amount of times Mr or Ms Sparky at interview turned out to be anything but in real life.

It took me many years to realise that if someone didn't fit in with us, then the sooner they went the better. The trouble with employing someone not suited to your business is that quite soon frustrations start appearing, then their confidence is shaken, and from then on it tends be nothing but a vicious downward spiral. I guess you always hope it will work out, and it's so much easier leaving things be than having to address them, but the amount of time and energy it ends up taking when someone is doing a bad job, or not getting on with their colleagues, is not to be underestimated. In addition to this, you might be doing them a favour as well as yourself, and they may well be much better suited to working in a different environment. To balance this, everyone goes through bad patches, and for this the opposite rule applies. There is no one, myself very much included, who wouldn't have been sacked at one point or another from our team if we had had a ruthless guru that we reported to. Sometimes you just have to bear with people, and see them through a difficult period. The skill, of course, lies in spotting the difference between a bad patch and a job done badly. Seham has an almost spooky ability to mind-read, and see what lies beneath the surface, and so I would increasingly rely on her judgement in these matters. She has an uncanny knack of knowing exactly when someone needs either a good clip round the ear, or a hug, and this became increasingly useful as time went on and we employed more people.

While Seham had been taking care of things so well at work, her domestic life had got into a bit of a mess. Typically, the main problem had stemmed from her good nature. Her sister had died about a year before, and Seham had clocked up thousands of pounds on telephone calls to Egypt consoling her niece. In addition to this were a host of other credit card and payment plan debts – the scourge of our society and it's criminally irresponsible that companies have been allowed to encourage people to take on debt so enthusiastically. It's ironic that we had a government that interfered in almost every aspect of our lives, and yet they allowed credit companies to encourage millions of people to get into crippling debt. No wonder it is now essential to avoid a full-blown credit crisis, or there'd be civil unrest up and down the country. Anyway, I spoke to James and asked if he could possibly look at how we might help Seham out of this hole. The trouble with debt is that when it gets beyond a certain threshold, it's tempting to give in and it just gets worse and worse. He was brilliant and negotiated with all the lenders and reduced her debt by about a third on the basis that we would pay that amount now, or the likelihood was that they would end up getting nothing. We did this and devised a plan for her to pay us back slowly. She had been so amazing to us for the past few years, working so hard and always with a huge smile on her face, that it was a real pleasure to be able to help her a little.

We now had a new problem to deal with, but this time it was a good one; we were running out of space. The big decision was where to look for new premises. The only large industrial estate near us was New Covent Garden Market, but they had no free units and so I started looking at Wimbledon. The price per foot would be a little cheaper there, and there were quite a few estates to choose from. The negative was that it was another 20–40 minutes' drive and we were still doing a lot of last-minute and emergency deliveries. These deliveries were one of our unique assets as we were the most centrally located sandwich supplier and could offer a level of service in London that was impossible for our competitors to match.

Just as I was looking, Danni mentioned that she was moving her company Tuck Box out of the top floor of our unit in Union Court. It was far from ideal, but we decided to take her space and move our office up a floor and turn the old office into an extension of our kitchen. The problem with sandwich production is storing the finished goods. Making them doesn't take up too much space. And so our old office became our new refrigerated allocation room and we had a lift put in to take the sandwiches upstairs to be allocated and labelled, and then down again and into the vans.

The other obvious advantage of this arrangement was that it was much cheaper than moving to new premises, and we still had another two years or so to go on the lease and so would have needed to try and sublet it if we had moved out.

The top floor actually made for a nicer office with a huge skylight giving it much more natural light than downstairs. By this point Maggie, who had been running our admin dept, and Gill in sales, had left us. Gill wanted to work nearer home and set up her own business (not sandwiches) and Maggie was going to go to Australia. The two had never got on, and it had taken all my diplomatic skills to keep the show on the road and them from each other's throats (Maggie had to deal with some of the problems we had with our clients, and this was naturally a sensitive area for Gill if she had introduced that client), but it was quite a shame as they were both brilliant at what they did and they provided us with just the skills we needed at the time we needed them most. Gill in particular had been outstanding, and her contribution when we were going through our toughest period was invaluable. I was discussing Maggie's new life in Australia with her one day and, calling on our experience in France, mentioned that life tended to go on much the same wherever you are, it was mainly the weather that changed. She came up with a classic line that I often quote. 'Oh yes,' she said, 'I'm very aware that I'm taking myself with me!'

We were doing a lot of business with the BBC at this time and, amongst others, we were also supplying the Royal Albert Hall, the Opera House, the Natural History Museum, Harrods, and the House of Commons, as well as Buckingham Palace – quite a cool client list by any standards . . . We had also started supplying Caffè Nero, a small coffee chain at the time with about seven outlets. They were growing fast and were a good client, but incredibly demanding and we were being pushed more and more to do bespoke products for them. By this time our product list had grown to about 130 different varieties of sandwich excluding any bespoke lines. It was so much easier adding to the menu than taking things away from it, and it naturally had become more and more extensive. I had a eureka moment one day when I popped into a Pret shop to buy a drink. I remember it clearly, and as I walked down Lower Regent Street afterwards I reflected on the fact that they only had about fourteen different varieties for sale. What on earth were we doing offering 130? Who could possibly want 130 different varieties on their shelf?

Seham and I went through our menu in detail and cut it down to 65 varieties. This would be very much less than any of our competitors and so a bit of a risk, but the upside was that we would have longer production runs, could con-centrate even more on quality control with less varieties to oversee and, critically, that we would change twelve to fifteen of our varieties every three months thereby providing a feeling of change and freshness to our offer.

It was quite a job making a change of this magnitude to our operation, deciding what to keep and what to ditch, and making sure we had time to use up all the ingredients of the varieties we were going to stop making. We also wanted to run it past our main clients first as a precaution and so the whole process took about three months. None of them objected and we introduced the new menu. What was incredible was that not a single other client objected to the new menu either, and in fact a lot of them thought we had done them a favour as making their order each day had become a less complex task. This was a huge lesson. We had been stretching ourselves to the limit providing what we thought and assumed our clients wanted, and we had been wrong. To be fair, in a lot of these things it is also probably how you ask the question. If we had asked everyone, I'm sure quite a few clients would have said they needed this or that sandwich to stay on the menu. As it was, having consulted our main clients and had their approval, we said, 'This is what we are doing, we hope it's OK with you,' to the rest. Changing the menu regularly was the clever bit. One of the things we sometimes came up against was a client wanting to change supplier because they wanted a change and something different to keep their customers happy. By having a menu change every three months we could weed out the less good selling lines and try something new and keep a constant sense of change around our offer. We had previously changed menu about once a year or 18 months and this was also the practice amongst most of our competitors. It also gave us the opportunity to take out products that were making a poor margin and replace them with something more profitable. We were in a period of ingredient cost deflation and so we never put our prices up during these years and our menu changes enabled us to manipulate our prices a little, although we always took pains to make sure that some new products were cheaper than the ones they had replaced as well. We knew the margin we wanted to achieve, but never abused this and never charged more than we needed to.

The other advantage of a regular menu change was that it provided us with something to talk about and an excuse to visit clients and keep in touch with them. It was one of the parts of my job I enjoyed the most, and I used to love going to see a client with a box of lovely new samples. We always made sure we had one quirky sandwich in a new menu that wouldn't sell much, but would provide some interest, and these always made good talking points. Mascerpone and pear with fresh mint on chocolate bread would be a typical example. Delicious since you ask . . .

We continued to try and find a sales director, but to no avail. However brilliant they may have appeared to be in their previous jobs, they couldn't get going with us and we tried two in as many years. I have to accept that maybe it was us, although I always stressed strongly that they would have to drive and motivate themselves. We worked at a hell of a pace at this time, made decisions quickly and then acted on them immediately. There was a constant buzz and never a dull moment. We may have been doing a much greater volume, but we still had endless operational issues to deal with and I would still be doing an emergency delivery most days. It got to the point where I almost didn't feel I'd done a full day's work if I hadn't been out on the road or rolled my sleeves up to do something – a bad habit, but I was still desperate to keep our overheads as low as possible, and it was easier for me as I knew how everything worked. Whether they found this environment intimidating or not I don't know, but the great thing with salesmen is that their performance is easier to judge than any other role and so, whatever the reason, no sales were no sales and they had to go.

By 2000 we were turning over £3m and were really motoring.

It was still incredibly hectic and we had to make the most of every opportunity, as we had no idea how long this golden patch would last. I remained constantly in fear that everything might go wrong, and was just as concerned as I had ever been if we screwed up, and everyone worked really hard to make sure every delivery went smoothly. I was very involved in almost every aspect of what we did – what would nowadays be called micromanaging – and found it very hard to let go. The exception was always the kitchen where Seham had taken complete control. We were now fully operating seven days a week with weekend deliveries to museums, theatres, airports, the BBC and others. Seham was working pretty much seven days a week as well, either at work, or on the end of the phone – a habit she would continue for the next few years, and if there was ever a problem at any time of day or night she was the one who would sort it out. In her I had found someone who was not only incredibly intelligent and wise, but who also who cared about the business as much as I did. It's not for nothing that I credit her with our success.

We were now using a third-party distribution company for our out-of-London deliveries. This was more cost effective than doing it ourselves, as they had vans going to similar places anyway. The problem was that it meant we lost some control, which I was never happy about, but had to learn to accept. There were inevitably some issues and one entire weekend when staying with my father in Hereford was taken up dealing with irate clients and trying to find a way of delivering to them. The deliveries through the distribution company we were using hadn't turned up because half the drivers hadn't pitched up for work as their boss was away on holiday. I asked Kamel from this time on to see what it would take to have an emergency back-up to the third-party company. I was quite used to the weekend being disturbed, as there was one issue or another every weekend, but never on a scale like that (sometimes it would be someone just wondering when their delivery was arriving, and other times wanting to increase or decrease their order for the next day), but what really upset me was letting our clients down. It was so hard to get to a position of winning business, and I was damned if we were going to lose any. As I had most of the contact with clients, it was natural that they would ring me in such emergencies.

For the past few years I had become obsessed with the business and would think about it the entire time, often waking in the middle of the night wondering if we had done this or that. There was so much going on with all the day-to-day work and part of my initial reasoning for starting the business had become true, that if the sandwiches were good, we would get repeat business. It was fantastic getting a wave of orders every day, but it also meant that there wasn't any time to pause and every day was a busy day.

We had recently recruited Rowan to our admin team and I suggested to Seham one day that maybe she could work helping me as a sort of PA. 'Don't be silly,' she said, 'you'd drive the poor girl mad if she was working all day with you.' I suggested we give it a go, and it certainly wouldn't be permanent if she wasn't happy. We proceeded to get on like a house on fire. It wasn't often I could prove Seham wrong and that was fun. Rowan was exactly what I needed and started organising me and bossing me about and taking away from me a lot of small things I had become in the habit of doing, but could just as easily be done by someone else. I quickly realised that I should have found someone to help me ages ago but, ridiculously, had been so busy that I hadn't even thought about it. Delegating was not my strong point at this stage and it took a lot of trust for me to let go of anything. As I began to do it, more and more I realised that people not only enjoyed being given more responsibility, but were more often than not much better at doing the task than I ever had been. It used to irritate me at the start of running my own business when I read in business books how important it was to delegate. It all sounds very well, but when you're a start-up business, and everyone is working flat out, there is no one to delegate to. The reality is that you have to get to a certain size before you have such a luxury. I heard a very neat quote just the other day for when the luxury of delegation can be afforded, however: 'I only do what only I can do'.

Taking the top floor had proved a very good move, although we went through stages of having a lot of problems with the lift breaking, and eventually had some of our staff trained in basic lift maintenance. Having to walk down two flights of stairs with thousands of sandwiches was not thought to be that much fun by the allocators. A problem did start to arise, though, when our landlord changed. The previous one had always been cooperative and had also appreciated that we were one of the first tenants on the estate. The representative of the new landlord was a different animal altogether, and desperate to see whatever additional bit of cash he could extract from us. It transpired we had a weakness that he was only too happy to exploit to the full. We had three car parking spaces that came with the unit. On these three spaces we had two large rubbish containers that were emptied daily. We had also had permission from the previous landlord to put a refrigerated container on the two parking spaces that had been allocated to the top floor when we took it over. Our weakness was that we had six vans and no written consent for the rubbish bins or container to be taking up the parking spaces. We had parked the vans on other available spaces and directly outside our unit and had never had a problem. I explained this to the new landlord, but he could see he was onto something and wasn't going to let go. He was a nasty little creep and I'd sometimes see him from my office paying a visit to the estate and walking around menacingly in a black trench coat. All of the other tenants grew to have a similar dislike of him and it was as if he had a hidden agenda to try and clear the estate of all tenants. We had a potentially huge problem now. If he insisted on us removing the refrigerated container (we used to store the sandwiches there prior to being loaded into vans, as we wouldn't have time to bring them down in the lift while the drivers waited) and not allow us to park our vans anywhere then we wouldn't be able to continue trading.

I completely loathed this man and everything he stood for, and he really got under my skin. One day he came to see me and said that if we paid them £10k they would give us a permit for the bins and the container, and allow us to park our vans as long as they weren't hindering anybody else. I said that was outrageous and we already had permission and that this was extortion. 'Well,' he replied, 'a similar thing happened to my father a few years ago, so I know how you feel, but that's the deal.' How could he do this to me when he had seen his father treated the same way? I just don't understand some people.

I paid the £10k. We had too much else going on, and I needed this risk removed.

One thing was for sure however, when our lease was up there was no way we were staying.

Looking back I realise that I took the whole thing far too personally and he was just being a tough and ruthless businessman, but at the time I felt like someone was trying to harm my baby and I deeply resented that and hated him for it.

It doesn't rain, but it pours, and at roughly the same time I had a call one day from the head office of one of our largest contract catering clients asking if they could come and see me. This company had become a very significant part of our business as they not only ran the catering for a lot of the companies in the City, but also many entertainment and sporting venues. They had also gone on a massive acquisition spree, swallowing up a lot of smaller contract caterers, some of which had been clients of ours and had kept using us. The sandwich buyer came to my office and we had a perfectly pleasant conversation, with him going to great pains to tell me what a terrific job we were doing, and how much more business might be available. 'This is going a little too well,' I thought to myself, just as he leant back and said, 'But we will need better prices from you. You are much more expensive than our other suppliers, you know.' 'Yes, and much better too,' I nearly said, but held myself back as I knew it was best not to get into any conversation about prices, and the sooner the subject changed the better. 'We can't do that, I'm afraid,' I said instead. 'Well, think about it and give me a ring,' he replied. The threat was clear, and it was more than just potential new business that was at risk.

Despite these hiccups along the way, we had a cracking year and had surged ahead to nearly £5.5m by mid-2001. This was beyond belief and so far ahead of my wildest dreams. It was hard to take in (still is actually) and we were making almost as much in a week as we had been in a whole year not so long ago. At around this time we were being pushed harder and harder by Caffè Nero as they expanded speedily, particularly into the provinces. They had become increasingly demanding regarding their product specifications, which I didn't mind so much, but, while the operations director that I generally dealt with was a great guy, his assistant was a pain in the arse and we were all quite keen to see the back of her.

I began to realise that it was great business when it tied in with the rest of our delivery routes, but it didn't make any sense if we had to drive miles to make one drop for them. I sat down with the operations director and explained that where they were going didn't fit in with our plans and said we would supply them for as long as it took them to find another supplier they were happy with. It had been good business and we parted very amicably but, once again, we had to clear the decks a bit to keep our operation as simple as we could and to enable us to offer an outstanding service to the rest of our clients.

We had also started supplying an interesting character who had set up a company called Foo-go. If ever anyone could sell ice to the Eskimos it was him and he had won a contract to supply WH Smith at transport outlets such as railway stations and airports. He was a great marketer and his idea was to be the middleman and buy in a whole range of food-to-go products, have them packaged in his branding, and offer a one-stop shop. WH Smith had previously worked with M&S but felt there was a conflict when M&S Simply Food outlets starting appearing in the same market. It was quite an interesting idea, but I was never sure how there was going to be enough margin to accommodate a third party such as him. He had used another supplier but had had quality issues and so we took it over. I was always slightly nervous as it became clear over time that while the guy running it was great at sales and marketing, he wasn't much of a businessman, but the concept went from strength to strength and we started making significant sales to them.

CHAPTER 8

First Attempt at Selling – A Close Call

As well as things were going, there was no time to rest on our laurels as our lease was coming to an end and I had to start thinking of where to go to next.

This was going to be a big decision and the last few years had been such an incredible roller-coaster I wasn't sure I had the stomach to risk everything we had made to fund expansion into an even bigger and better facility. Perhaps it was time to hand the reins over to a fresh pair of hands and sell up to a larger company. The appeal of this option was pretty big. We had had a good run recently after a sustained tough period and I could for the first time in my life get a bit of cash and actually have a breather. I could even possibly keep my job, but not have all the responsibility. It was sounding better and better, and I engaged a small company in the City that specialised in finding buyers for companies. They introduced me to a potential buyer from Cornwall. It was a crisp company that had some funding and were keen to grow by acquisition. They thought we might be a neat fit and we could sell and distribute their crisps in our vans as well as provide them with a London base. It was run by a very charismatic entrepreneur, we got on well, and discussions began in earnest.

Meanwhile, on the home front we had moved out of the flat and done up (or more accurately, Harriet had done up) and moved into a house on the other side of Clapham Common. Soon after moving in there in late 1998 we decided it would be fun to spend the Easter term in the Alps. All Lycées had the same curriculum and so it was possible to leave one school and go to another and carry on doing exactly the same course. We rented a tiny two-bedroom studio apartment down the hill from Chatel in the French Alps and Harriet and the younger two spent the term there while I went out as often as I could, which in reality turned out to be very rarely as I was so busy back at the ranch. Such a pity and a real waste, as it was a unique opportunity, but foolish of me to ever think I would have the time to get away much at this stage. The drive up the mountain early in the morning was the all-time great school run though, and breathtakingly beautiful on a nice day. We had rented out two bedrooms in the house in Clapham to help subsidise the rent of the apartment and that was a huge mistake. I had two young people living in my house and I had assumed they would be out and about and I wouldn't see much of them. Incredibly, they only went out about three times the whole time they were there. I couldn't believe it, and loathed having my space so invaded and counted down the days till they left. We had also taken the decision to put Sasha into an English private school for the next academic year, having seen the incredible benefits Jimbo had enjoyed. The French education system is excellent, but if it had a fault in our eyes it was that it was very harsh. Pastoral care would, in every sense, be foreign words to the teachers we experienced, especially in London, and then it was all the other things around the edges such as music and art and theatre and sport. In short, it would be a nicer way for her to be educated if we could afford it, and we began to think that maybe we could.

I went to book a tennis court on the Common one Sunday a year or so later and I dreamed about how incredible it would be if we had a house in the country and had our own court (there's nothing wrong with ambition). We had been trying to find a house nearby that had off-street parking as we would sometimes have to park a few roads away when we returned from going out to dinner. There were a few, but they cost a fortune. I came back from booking the court and told Harriet of my idle thoughts and we thought we'd have a quick look on the internet to see what was available in the country. We didn't know where to start and so put in Hampshire and gaily scrolled down the list of properties available that were in order of price, ending up going far further than we could afford, as the way tends to be in such things. We then came across an artist's impression of an attractive-looking house near Andover, wherever that was. 'No harm in going to see it,' we thought, once we'd found it on the map, and we could pop in on Harriet's parents on the way down. It was beautiful countryside, there were only the foundations to look at, but we fell in love with the view. This impulse had sent us down quite a path. If we were going to go down it, though, we would need to borrow a lot of money and the Lloyds Bank call centre in Scotland weren't going to be able to help me. I rang the friend whose house I had stayed in all those years ago when we were living in France – only four in fact, but it felt like a lifetime – and asked him who he suggested I speak to. He immediately gave me HSBC Private bank's telephone number and a name and said they were the people to talk to. (Bear with me at this stage, there is a point to this story.) I went for a meeting with the contact he had suggested and we were joined by another rather older colleague. We had a good meeting and I agreed to show them our company accounts as any loan would have to be against the company. When I looked at the business cards they had given me later I saw that the older man was Marcus Gregson, the chief executive of the bank. I never found out what he was doing at that meeting, but it was probably just him being curious. I had explained that I was in the process of selling Daily Bread, and so I hoped the loan wouldn't be a long-term one, and we would of course sell our house in Clapham as soon as the one in Andover was built. Once they had seen the Daily Bread accounts they agreed to make the loan and so things were progressing pretty well. It was a busy time, but this was good fun compared with most of the busy times I was used to, and I went to the bank for another meeting with Harriet as Marcus wanted to make sure he knew exactly who they were lending to.

Negotiations continued well with the crisp company and we had arrived at an agreed valuation and they were coming down to London to go through some final details. I was meeting them at 12noon and had agreed to drop in on Marcus at HSBC at 10am as he said he wanted a chat. He sat me down, looked me in the eye and said, 'You cannot sell this company. You're tired and completely exhausted and you don't know what you're doing. You've worked your arse off all these years just to give your company away.' I couldn't believe how strongly he felt and, apart from anything else, I was touched by his real concern. How could he be so certain? His team had looked at our figures and heard our story and reckoned we could grow the company into something at least four times its current size, and then showed me the effect that would have on any multiple a buyer might be prepared to subsequently pay. They were dazzling numbers, but there could be no certainty, and what about a bird in the hand? At least he made me promise not to commit to anything at the meeting later that day. I arrived at my meeting in the City and immediately told the team that had arrived from Cornwall that all bets were off and that I needed time to think. Not popular, but there we were.

And so I came not to sell Daily Bread in 2001. Apart from not closing the business down in 1997, it was the best financial decision I ever made, and entirely down to Marcus Gregson, who just happened to be sitting in on a meeting with one of his assistant directors when I went for my first meeting at the bank. He subsequently became quite a mentor to me and continued to show huge interest in how we fared. This endorsement and encouragement from a major City figure for both my business and myself was an enormous confidence boost. He also has a rapier wit and great sense of humour, and we have had lunch pretty much every six months from that day to this. Top man.

CHAPTER 9

New Covent Garden Market

So, back to looking for our next premises. Wimbledon was still the obvious place to look and I spent a lot of time visiting industrial estates trying to find one within easy distance of public transport. There was no point having somewhere that staff would struggle to get to. The more difficult requirement, though, was trying to find somewhere with sufficient space outside for our rubbish bins and vans. I wasn't going to have the same problem again. I spoke to everyone I could think of, including some people that worked in New Covent Garden Market, but they all told me it was fully let and there was a list as long as your arm of companies wanting to move there. I thought I'd contact the Market Authority that ran the estate anyway, just to hear it from the horse's mouth. It turned out a large fruit and veg company had just gone bust and some space might be available. There were twelve units available, and how much space did we want? I never knew what happened to the list of potential tenants, and it was probably just market gossip. The units were each 1300 sq ft and so we reckoned nine units would be perfect, giving us 12,000 sq ft instead of the 5000 (including the top floor) we currently had. We didn't want too much space as it was hard to know how much additional demand there would be in our now semi-niche market.

Everything was proceeding smoothly until another company already trading on the estate said they might be interested in taking some of the space. It soon got to the point where we would have to go to sealed bids. We would be paying the same rent as everyone else, but whoever offered the biggest premium up front would get the units. It was impossible to know how much to pay: £10k? £50k? £100k? It was a perfect place for us to be with endless space for bins and parking, as well as being in a fantastic location. Just as importantly as all this was the fact that it was only about half a mile from Union Court and so we wouldn't lose any staff in the move. I was determined to move there by now. I eventually managed to find out that the other interested party was a cheese company and went to see them. It turned out they didn't want all the space and we agreed to compromise and split the units and take six each. We would have to do the same as we had at Union Court and build a mezzanine floor to get the space we needed, and, just as we completed the work, the cheese company pulled out and decided they didn't need the space after all. Well, at least we hadn't paid a huge premium to be there.

We had been incredibly busy at Union Court and were really bursting at the seams in the last year or so. The great thing about this was that it enabled us to build up cash to fund the expansion into the new premises and therefore de-risk the move to quite an extent. We did also badly need a new, larger and better-equipped facility, not just to enable us to continue to expand, but also to meet the ever-increasingly stringent standards we had to work to. We were getting inspected more and more by our bigger clients and needed to have a state of the art kitchen to meet their demands and to pass their audits. It was much easier doing up the units than Union Court had been because we could now afford to get a professional building contractor involved, rather than just me and an architect, and it all went much more smoothly.

We built a mezzanine floor over the entire unit and so were a bit top heavy with more space than we needed upstairs. It did enable us to build a huge staff room and also create a large dry goods storeroom for packaging, labels, spare crates etc as well as a nice office. The office was open plan with a meeting room and a small office for me. I had suggested maybe having my desk in the open-plan office, but Seham had become increasingly bossy by now and reckoned I would meddle and interfere less if I was tucked away and out of harm's way.

The move itself was pretty stressful. We persuaded all our weekend clients not to have a Sunday delivery, thereby freeing up our Saturday production. The sandwiches all had two days life on them, so a large order on Friday for Saturday delivery would see them through in an emergency. We then had to move every single piece of equipment, conveyor belts, buttering machines and so on from the kitchen, and every-thing from our offices, on the Friday night and Saturday morning, and hope that it all worked by Saturday evening, ready for Sunday production – our busiest day of the week. We had engineers with us to move and set up all the kitchen equipment and make sure it was running OK, and it had to be. We couldn't afford to let everyone down on the Monday morning. All key kitchen staff and all of the office staff came in and spent the whole weekend packing up and unpacking everything and then setting it up. Even the telephone lines were critical as almost all our orders were by phone and so we were pretty vulnerable if BT let us down switching over lines. As we had stayed in a similar area ever since we moved into our own premises in Sleaford Street in 1987, we had managed to keep the same telephone number since then.

Everything worked. It really was amazing, but the whole move went without a hitch and we quickly settled in. I always have to be able to visualise things before making a big decision, and had easily imagined us working in the Market, the hustle and bustle, ingredients being delivered, our vans being loaded and setting off, even down to parking my car and walking up the stairs to the office in the morning. It was exactly as I dreamt, and the good news was that we could now have a hundred vans if we wanted, and still have room to park them all. And no little shit was going to tell us we couldn't. I eventually came to be grateful to the Union Court landlord as it became increasingly clear what a great place to work the Market was, and we might well have been tempted to take some extra space in Union Court if it hadn't been for their attitude. It's funny how often something that seems a nightmare at the time ends up being a blessing eventually.

Meanwhile things on the Andover front were not going so well. The house was meant to have been finished in time for us to move in for Christmas 2001. It then moved, in a nice seasonal way, to Easter and then changed on a monthly basis thereafter. We were going to be moving the business in July 2002 and so I initially had seven months leeway between the two moves. The last thing I needed was moving house and work at the same time, and we were heading more and more onto a collision course. As it turned out, we moved into Covent Garden exactly on schedule, and the week later we moved into the house in Andover. The builder hasn't remained on our Christmas card list, but we have enjoyed living in the house he eventually built.

We had slowed our growth over the previous year and turnover stayed pretty much the same at around £5.5m. As far as I was concerned that was fine and things could be a lot worse, but a business is like pond water and must keep moving or it goes stagnant. If we weren't growing we would lose momentum and as soon as we did that we would run the risk of starting to lose business, and we knew all too well how that felt. One of the other big lessons in the Anthony Robbins book was how everything we do is governed by subconsciously moving away from pain and towards pleasure. Of course it then depends on what we associate with pain and pleasure. A classic example would be smoking which can be either an enjoyable thing to do, or an awful thing to do to your health, and smelly and expensive etc. It depends which side of this crude fence you sit on, and your attitude will determine the outcome. If someone wanted to give up smoking, for instance, but still felt it was an enjoyable thing to do, they would exercise great restraint and deny themselves this pleasure, the chances are they will fall back into it sooner or later. However, if their overriding thought is that it's a bad thing to do and has pain attached to it, then they will naturally lean away from it and stop. For those that know it's bad and want to stop, but carry on anyway, it is because, deep down, they still associate more pleasure to the experience than pain.

Anyway, to use the pain/pleasure example, I was now more driven by the pain of failure than the pleasure of success. I would take care of the downside and the upside would take care of itself. It would matter if we started losing business, and it didn't matter how much we grew.

While we had been busy minding our own business, there had been a lot of consolidation in our industry. We had had about eight competitors for the previous few years, three large ones and the rest smaller. Quite a few small ones had come and gone in the meantime, mainly falling down by being seduced by volume and discounting their prices to get it, or offering sale and return to garages and similar outlets – the road to ruin if ever there was one. To give people your products who don't really care if they sell them or not, and then have all the administration of working how many you put in and how many unsold ones you had picked up each day seemed suicide to me, and generally was. An interesting example of a different type was experienced by those companies supplying a major petrol station group that had outsourced their sandwich buying to a third-party company which gave the business to whichever manufacturer they thought best. From what we could gather, it wasn't sale and return, but they could dictate which suppliers to use, and thereby the price they had to pay for many of their ingredients. The volumes were enormous, I would guess at least 10,000 sandwiches a day and company after company got into trouble supplying them, having ended up not being able to make any margin. This was exactly the sort of business we were keen to avoid, and we made sure we concentrated all our efforts on finding full margin business, as even reducing our prices by a tiny amount would mean we would have to work much harder to make the same profit.

Now that we were in our smart new kitchens, I thought it was time we started marketing ourselves better and I had a new logo designed. Unlike the first logo that we had used up until that point, this was to be a professional job and I was put in touch with a small, very creative design company called Bigfish. They came up with various different options and I went with the most radically different design from our original one. I was by now keen to try and develop Daily Bread as a brand, and wanted to make us stand out even more from our competitors. By developing a brand I hoped we might move further away from our products being treated as a commodity, and as well as developing more loyalty from our end consumers

In June 2002, just before we moved to New Covent Garden, I thought I would look into how Royal Warrants worked. We had now been supplying Buckingham Palace for about five years and I wondered if it might be possible for us to apply for a Warrant. The Palace put me onto the Royal Warrant Holders Association and they sent me some forms to fill in, which I duly returned to them. I was told it would take about six months to process the application. I was really hoping this would succeed as, apart from anything else, a Royal Warrant would sit perfectly next to our new logo. By December I had asked Rowan to look out for any correspondence from Buckingham Palace and, just before Christmas, I had a very smart crested envelope in my hands. This was a big moment – a Royal Warrant would cement our reputation as a top-quality supplier and be a wonderful endorsement for us – and, apart from this, no other sandwich company had ever held a Royal Warrant.

'We are pleased to confirm . . . ' I have rarely been more excited and immediately went and announced the news to the rest of the office. We had, in a sense, arrived at last, and we could now really get going re-branding the company and having new letterheads, van livery and labels made with the new logo and Warrant.

Branding had become important as we were keen to stand out from the crowd and while making sandwiches might not be the most exotic of industries, we were determined to try and at least make it a bit more funky. I also wanted to add a bit of character to the brand, and we started printing quotes on the back of our sandwich labels. These would change every week and were designed to make the reader smile (and occasionally, to think) and were typically from Oscar Wilde, Groucho Marx, Mark Twain and so on. Because we were wholesaling, the consumer was not directly our customer, and yet they were the people we wanted to appeal to. Apart from liking our sandwiches, I wanted them to like us, so that in turn they would be loyal to us and be keen for their caterer to continue using us rather than maybe switching to an alternative supplier.

As part of the consolidation of the sandwich 'food service' (i.e. non-retail) industry a new company appeared at this time called Food Partners. This was a shell company formed with venture capital money and their idea was to create a national company that could supply anywhere in the UK. To do this they did a deal to become the main sandwich supplier to one of the major contract caterers. They then went around the country offering to buy the companies that were currently large suppliers to that caterer. They either sold to Food Partners, or lost their biggest client, so it was quite an easy decision, and it was a ruthless but masterful way of picking up comparatively cheap businesses. We were one of three suppliers of premium sandwiches in London at the time and they had soon bought one of the others, encouraged by the fact that they not only did quite a lot of business with the caterer, but also had a very lucrative contract to supply Costa Coffee.

At the beginning of 2003 we recruited David Singh, a salesman from one of the companies Food Partners had bought. He didn't like the new regime and, having come across our name more and more, he approached us. He was an exception to the previous salesmen we had tried and, contrary to them, loved getting out and about and meeting new people and getting new business. David's style was much more the cheeky chappy approach than we would normally go for, but his boundless enthusiasm and good humour more than made up for this, and he was just what we needed as we were getting more and more enquiries. We relied quite a bit on catering managers moving from site to site for their companies and they would ring us at their new unit and ask us to supply them there. Either that, or they would refer us to their colleagues in other units. We had by now developed a small client liaison team to make sure we offered a really good service and looked after any operational issues, and either the client liaison manager or David or myself would go out in response to these enquiries. It was a wonderful feeling driving back from a good meeting where the catering manager had said what great things they'd heard about us and how much they looked forward to using us, and it really felt like we were beginning to get on top of our game. We also regularly had feed-back from new clients that their sandwich business had increased after switching to us and this added to our confidence, as well as giving us another valuable selling point for future potential clients.

By this stage we were beginning to appear on the radar of our competitors as we were taking so much business from them, and they had in turn starting creating more exotic sandwiches and developing a premium range of their own to help them compete with us. They were much larger companies than us, though, and much more cumbersome in their whole operation, and so it was quite easy for us to stay one step ahead and we constantly came up with new ideas, and new recipes, as well as point of sale promotions and general improvements to our service. Our killer weapon continued to be the quarterly new menu and, as soon as we launched a new menu, Seham would set to work creating sandwiches for the next one. She had a great ability to come up with ideas for new sandwiches that were also commercially viable, and she and I worked closely, refining the recipes until they were exactly as we wanted them.

I decided to join an interesting sounding group that a

friend had mentioned to me. They were called the Academy of Chief Executives (ACE). An awful name and I would never have gone near them if it wasn't for the recommendation. I went for a trial day and joined a group of ten other men and women, all of whom ran their own businesses, some small, and some large. They were a very dynamic lot and the format was to have a speaker in the morning and then discuss members' issues round the table during the afternoon. The speaker on that first day was fascinating and I have found his tips useful from that day.

He taught us how to breathe. It soon became apparent that there was a bit more to it than meets the eye. First of all he put a ring on one of the group's finger. The ring was wired to his computer and this enabled us to see his heart rate on the image projected onto the screen. He then asked this person to not say anything, but to think about something that was bothering or upsetting him at the time. His heart rate immediately leapt up. It was incredible to watch, as there he was sitting in front of us looking exactly the same. The speaker then asked him to mentally re-join the group while the rate normalised. After a few minutes he asked the same guy to now breath in deeply for five seconds, hold it for five seconds, and exhale for five seconds and while he did this, to think of something pleasant. His heart rate once again immediately changed, this time dramatically slowing. We were told this was a useful tool, to be used whenever one wanted to calm down, and particularly when frustrated in traffic, nervous before a meeting, or in similar situations. I personally find it very useful when we're running late and my wife's just given the wrong directions when I'm driving. An invaluable tool.

In the afternoon we would go round the table and everyone would say how their month had gone and raise any issues that were concerning them. It was obviously very important that there be no conflict of interest amongst any of the members' businesses. The chairman would then suggest the three or so main issues that seemed the most pressing and we would address them. First of all the person with the issue would spell out in as much detail as possible the exact details surrounding it. Then the rest of the group would have 20 minutes or so to ask further questions to get a really clear understanding. Once there was total clarity regarding the nature, the consequences, and the potential future consequence of the problem, we would go round the table in turn offering our advice. What most staggered me was how honest people were. I'd never heard a group of people be so candid with each other and, on a good day, it was incredibly powerful and we had some amazing discussions. Often someone had a contact that could be useful in helping solve an issue that had been raised. It was a business group, but occasionally a personal issue would be raised and we would try and deal with that, as it is all linked. There were times when the atmosphere was electric and where we collectively felt we had been able to make a significant difference. I really enjoyed these monthly sessions, mainly because I had a lot of respect for the rest of the group and their views. It also provided a very good opportunity to get out of the office and spend the day in a different, but very stimulating environment.

What the ACE group mainly had in common was a real desire to learn and we had some great speakers occasionally that really were quite inspirational. Rebecca Stephens, the first British woman to climb the Seven Summits was one, and another man had coached Clive Woodward, the England rugby coach. Working as a team, having a common objective, only as good as the weakest link etc. One lesson I remember resonating very clearly was of the England player that was a great kicker of the ball, but not so good at passing. He had spent months working on improving his passing, until his new coach advised him to just accept he was never going to be the best passer of the ball, and to instead concentrate on really honing his kicking skills and being brilliant at that. Concentrate on what you're good at.

A nice Woodward story also rang true: the England squad would meet up regularly and attend meetings together. When Woodward arrived he couldn't believe how many players arrived a few minutes late, or the meeting was interrupted by mobiles ringing and so on. At the end of his first meeting he had a word with them all and said what he felt about time keeping etc, and asked them to give it some thought and come back the following week with their own solution. They were all there when he arrived for the next meeting and they explained their new rules to him. No mobiles in the training ground, or even inside hotels – they would have to leave the building to use their phones at all, and from now on anything less than ten minutes early for a meeting or training session was deemed to be late and they would be fined and given a really hard time by their fellow players. He had improved discipline in one fell swoop but, crucially, this discipline had been self-imposed by the team – and as a result was probably much tougher than anything he would have tried to impose on them. The lesson made a lot of sense to me; if we could get our staff to work together and impose discipline on each other, through fear of letting each other down, then that could only be a good thing.

Seham and I had always loathed time clocks for stamping people in and out of work and, despite many people advising us that we should get one as we grew larger, we wouldn't dream of it. Everything about them is wrong in my mind. If you can't trust people, they shouldn't be employed, and if they don't trust you, then they shouldn't work for you, and if your managers can't maintain discipline including time keeping, then they shouldn't be managers. The most important part of the culture Seham developed was in getting our staff to take care of each other. As soon as they cared for each other, they wouldn't want to be late, or off sick, or letting the side down in any way. Peer pressure would end up being much more powerful than anything we could try to impose. We did, however, try to lead from the front and always tried to take care of all our staff. Seham had grown into a role as half mother and half sergeant major to the kitchen staff. She would look after you and take care of you and do anything for you if were reliable and worked hard, and God help you if you thought you could get away with shirking or taking the piss in any way. Seham had to deal with masses of personal issues that people brought to her, sometimes awful problems, and in extremes she would mention an issue to me and ask if there was anything we could do to help. We had a policy by now of never lending money to staff. It is easy to lend money, but then, apart from anything else, you feel pretty bad about asking them to repay it, and it's debatable how much of a favour you are doing them in the first place. Much easier to say no, we have a policy. If we wanted to give someone some money, then we did just that and gave it to them in the form of a discretionary bonus. We did also pay for one of our supervisor's flights back to Ghana to attend her mother's funeral on one occasion, and various other one-off contributions. Although these things were not done to be shouted about, the ripple effect on the rest of the staff hearing that we really did care was immeasurable.

We were really steaming ahead at this stage and week after week we would ship in some pizzas for lunch on Friday to celebrate yet another record turnover. We also now had the resources to buy new vans and only run them for three years before replacing them as well as investing in good computer back-up systems, shadow servers and so on. The reality was that, like almost any business nowadays, we were pretty stuffed if our computers ever failed, and so we invested increasingly in reducing this risk.

Moving to bigger premises is always a risk and the fear is naturally that if it coincides with losing a major client, then the whole business could be jeopardised. We couldn't have been more fortunate in this move, and business had continued to pour in, taking us to over £7.8m by July 2003.

I thought it was worth another stab at getting a really good salesman on board. We had been very fortunate, the market had moved in our favour and we had benefited from a lot of referral work, but we couldn't go on relying on it forever and again the thought was if we were doing this well without a dynamo heading our sales, what could we achieve if we did? I thought we would chuck some money at the problem this time and we used a head-hunter to recruit someone. We would offer a good salary and an exciting incentive package that could double that salary and see if that worked. We ended up with two candidates and decided to go with one who had been put on the fast-track management-training programme by Rank Hovis McDougall. He had worked for British Bakeries amongst others, appeared very driven and energetic and, at last, we seemed to have our man.

We now had our gleaming new huge kitchens, a top salesman on board and nothing was going to stop us. And nothing would have stopped us if he had gone out and sold our products. He was much happier instead requesting endless historic sales data from Terry and compiling charts and analysis of who we had supplied and who had grown and who had shrunk, and what percentage exactly was that growth etc., etc. I wonder if this isn't the problem with a lot of large companies. As long as the department you are working in is doing OK you can sit back and make pretty graphs and endless in-depth performance analyses and all is well with the world. Well, not in our company it wasn't. We wanted action and we wanted new sales, and we wanted them as soon as possible to help us take advantage of our position in this exciting new market. The problem with salesmen is that, while they might not necessarily be good at selling sandwiches, they were generally quite good at selling themselves and so three months would go by and that was fine because it was the 'settling in, getting to know the business' period. Then after a few more months it would start becoming clear that their early rhetoric had been exactly that, and was not followed up with any sales. Then you hope – and they persuade you – that there is some exciting new business in the pipeline, and the next thing you know is that you have spent a lot of money and don't have a single sale to speak of after six months. And, worse than that, the potential new business looked like it was going to remain permanently potential. By this time their lack of performance would have become my main concern and it was time for another difficult conversation to discuss what other business they may be best suited to working in.

CHAPTER 10

Full Steam Ahead

Our one remaining independent London competitor, a company called Oldfields, had recently moved into a huge new facility – over 100k sq ft, which was close to ten times the size of their previous kitchens. They had been doing a pretty good job and had grown quickly, benefiting from the same market conditions as us, but this was a gigantic move. I think they may have been talking to one of the big supermarket chains and had thought there was a big chunk of new business to be had. This was pretty tempting as our businesses both involved lots of small orders and deliveries and the idea of having a huge order was of course attractive. But it had its dangers, and soon after moving in they realised they weren't getting the business they had hoped for and were desperate for any new business to help fill their factory. They started taking on anything for anyone and had to compromise on both quality and service and still couldn't find the necessary volume to pay for their new facility, eventually having to sell to a large food group that wanted their gleaming new factory. They had had a good business, but over-ambition ended up killing it.

We naturally benefited from this fall-out, and we found ourselves in the incredible position of only having one main competitor, in the form of the Food Partners conglomerate. It was quite easy for us, a much smaller concern, to differentiate ourselves from them as a business and we found ourselves growing at a very comfortable pace. Enough to keep us busy and on our toes, but not at such a rate that the wheels might start to come off. Perhaps we didn't need a sales supremo after all. I certainly didn't want to get to the stage where we were running faster than we could cope with, and possibly letting people down. We continued to try and simplify our operations as much as possible and otherwise kept our heads down and just carried on going as we were.

Foo-go had become a very significant client by now, representing nearly 25 per cent of our turnover, which was both a good and a bad thing. The business was great, but the credit risk was increasing all the time as they expanded throughout the country into more WH Smith shops. They were meant to pay us within 45 days, but this could easily become 60 days if their accounts department dragged things out and by this stage they could be owing us as much as £250k. I tend to make almost every major decision on instinct, and have come to learn that it is far from just a hunch that enters one's head occasionally, but instead a summary of all one's experiences to date, and not to be dismissed lightly. I just didn't feel comfortable continuing to supply them, and was increasingly terrified about the risk – they felt to me like an accident waiting to happen.

So, what had triggered this instinct? In all our discussions over the years the owner's enthusiasm for his business was undoubted, but cost never came into the discussion (for, say, new ingredients, or packaging labels) unless I raised it, and explained the impact it would have on prices. He was, quite simply, not a businessman in my mind. And besides, I had a reasonably established business by now and drove a four-year-old car, and his business was quite new, and clearly not making a fortune, and he drove a brand new Range-Rover – a worry even at the best of times. Most people can be categorised as being either best suited to working for themselves, or for others, and he was without doubt in the latter category. He was incredible at sales and marketing but was not commercial enough to be in charge of the purse strings. He would have been brilliant as part of a larger company, but I felt he was a danger if left to his own devices. There was no doubt about WH Smith's ability to pay them, but there was no telling how much money Foo-go were spending and therefore their ability to pay us. I sat down with the owner and said they were going in a different direction from us and we wanted to concentrate on our core business and we would continue to supply them until they had found another supplier, but would like it to happen within the next three months. Despite the fact that they were one of our largest clients, I wasn't prepared to risk trading with anyone I didn't have faith in, and sales mean nothing at all unless they are paid for. We had already discussed whether they could pay us sooner, and they claimed they were unable to, and so that avenue was closed. They found a new supplier within a couple of months, and it was quite a relief when their final payment came through, albeit £10k short, which was disappointing but small beer compared to the risk I felt we had been taking. We discussed the £10k shortfall (due to label and packaging origination costs) and I finally agreed to compromise and accept £5k to settle the account, but despite a personal assurance this was never paid. They ended up continuing for much longer than I thought they would, using various other manufacturers before finally being taken over by their supplier about five years later.

I was by now beginning to really enjoy our success and had slowly stopped feeling that we were just going through a lucky phase, and had become much better at backing off from the day-to-day. In fact, the more I let go, the better things seemed to go, and the more responsibility our senior staff had, the more they enjoyed their roles. My PA, Rowan, had taken a lot away from me, and it made me realise the benefit of having time to think and plan, rather than endlessly react and fire fight. It was impossible not to still worry about the business though, and I kept pushing hard for us to keep on improving. As we had grown we had built up a strong team in both the kitchen and the office, and so it had become a more fun place to work and it was therefore easier recruiting good new staff. A big part of the selection process was about whether we thought a new recruit would get on well with their colleagues, as one bad egg could have an enormous influence on the atmosphere. By this stage we were employing about twenty people in the office and about 180 in the kitchens. For office staff recruitment Seham and I developed our walk test. We would notice how fast an interviewee walked from the entrance of our office across to the meeting room for the interview. Slow walkers work slowly was our sophisticated theory. It wasn't foolproof, but gave us as good a guide as any we reckoned, and livened up our decision-making process: 'Yes I know they have the right skills and qualifications . . . but, oh dear, did you see the walk?' We had also moved a long way from the days of having to put up with bad behaviour for fear of losing someone, and Seham took no prisoners if anyone was becoming disruptive or not pulling their weight in either the office or the kitchen. If anyone was rude or abusive to either their colleagues or supervisors they would be sent home immediately for anything from a day to a week unpaid. I was told many years later that this apparently isn't legal – well, it should be, because it works and people very soon fell in line, and it played a big part in helping us create a close and tight-knit team that would do anything to help each other.

We had continued to grow sales through the large contract caterers. Their larger units were still run at this stage pretty autonomously, so as long as their margins were OK and their clients were happy, then they had a large degree of freedom as to which companies they used to supply their sandwiches or other goods. As a result, our relationship was almost exclusively with the unit managers, and we had very few dealings with their head offices or central purchasing departments. This began to change, with catering companies increasingly wanting to exert more control over how their units were managed, and seeing how they could leverage their purchasing power by using fewer suppliers. Individual unit managers knew how different we were, and therefore why it was worth paying a small premium for our goods, whereas a central purchasing manager would simply see a more expensive price list on their desk. It therefore became even more important for us to differentiate ourselves from our competitors.

We started looking at every aspect of our business with renewed vigour and employed a design company to come up with some new point-of-sale material to help us get our messages across to the catering units' customers – the end consumers. We always tried to avoid clichés as everyone banged on about using the finest, freshest ingredients etc (and don't even get me started on the word 'passion'; I bought an accessory for a hosepipe the other day and even that had been 'made with passion'). Instead we concentrated on things such as all our eggs being free-range – when it was still comparatively unusual – everything being handmade, and our regular menu changes as well as new sandwich of the month and so on. Ultimately, if their customers were happy, then it would be quite a risk for the unit manager to use another supplier. A big part of our role was to make the unit manager's life easy, and by having the sandwiches always arriving on time and without any quality issues meant he or she could get on with the rest of their duties uninterrupted.

I always said that about 50 per cent of the reason anyone used us was for our service, and 50 per cent for the quality of our sandwiches, and so we now had to look at how we could improve both these areas and take them to another level. Every week we would inspect and taste a selection of sandwiches randomly taken from the kitchen. These would be marked according to appearance, taste, consistency, fill level and freshness. Any notes would be immediately given to the kitchen manager who could make the suggested changes straight away. We would also do a monthly test benchmarking our sandwiches against High Street retailers and sandwich shops and, if we could persuade a friendly unit manager to give us some, our competitors' sandwiches. These tests were always interesting and we were continually amazed at how good many of the sandwiches looked, and how poor they tasted – either because of the ingredients, or simply through lack of seasoning. I used to love this process, as it either confirmed that we were as good as we thought we were, or gave us some good ideas as to how we could improve. We were always very critical of our own sandwiches and happy to change them if someone else was making a better version of a similar sandwich.

At around this time, inspired by a desire to do something for the Tsunami disaster relief fund, we also introduced a charity sandwich which had an additional sticker on it pledging 10p from the sale of the sandwich to the charity. We put this on one of our most popular varieties, and raised approximately £25k over a year. We continued to do this, supporting different charities over the following years, which gave us another small point of difference with our competitors, and also acted as another good staff morale booster.

The logistics of our business had by now become quite complicated. We were running departments covering admin, production, technical, transport, sales/client liaison and finance, employing over 200 people and having to allocate our sandwiches to over 700 separate accounts, and make approximately 300 deliveries on time every day. We took on some more staff to help in the admin dept as we had found that to be the best recruitment method for us. The admin dept took care of taking orders, dealing with small day-to-day issues with clients and processing production sheets, printing labels etc. If one of them was doing an outstanding job and clearly had potential to go further, we would put them into the client liaison dept where they would have greater responsibilities and spend time talking to clients, visiting them when necessary and opening new accounts. With the exception of our technical manager and our accounts dept, all our senior positions had been filled by people coming through the ranks, in both the office and the kitchen, as well as transport. The advantages of this was that they were a known quantity, had done an outstanding job in a pretty repetitive role, and we of course knew that they fitted in well with all their colleagues and made a generally positive contribution to the company. Their heart was in the right place.

We lost a few contract clients due to their purchasing department's influence, and I lost count of the amount of times I had to walk out of meetings having reached an impasse when I was threatened with losing all our business if we didn't reduce our prices. I always stuck to my guns regarding prices, arguing that if I could have reduced them I would have done so already, and took strength from that fact that I knew we were doing a great job, and also the fact that if I conceded that year, it would be a slippery slope and I would be having identical conversations *every* year until there was no margin left at all. On the other hand, we were very clear on the margins we wanted to achieve and never charged more than we needed to, in an effort to always offer good value. There were also several times when we could easily have put our prices up, but didn't, for instance when we knew our competitors had screwed up and catering units *had* to use us.

If we did lose a unit, they would very often come back to us after a couple of months as they hadn't been happy with the new supplier that had been imposed on them, and we touched wood and kept our heads down and carried on. We had raised our game in response to the threat, and our changing menu enabled us to speedily introduce any new ideas or products to our clients, maintaining a constant pace of change and innovation – something almost impossible for our larger competitor to copy. Our entire sales strategy was now to try and keep all our existing large clients, but to dilute them by building up the rest of our business and finding new clients. One of the problems we faced was that there was a lot of consolidation in the catering industry, with the large caterers buying up a lot of the smaller ones, and so this added to our challenge all the time.

Another opportunity also arose at this time through a company called SSP. They ran most of the catering and retail outlets in train stations throughout the country. Their managing director Chris Copner had heard of us, liked what we stood for and was determined to improve the sandwich offer at the stations they had outlets in. They had been making their own sandwiches up to this point but their kiosks and shops were looking pretty dated and we did a lot of work with their team designing a new shop. We would provide the sandwiches, it would be branded as Daily Bread and SSP would run it and buy all the other food and drink they wanted to sell. We trialled it at Charing Cross station with the idea that, if it worked, we could roll the concept out throughout the country. It was an incredible opportunity for us to develop a nationwide brand, and would be risk-free for us as SSP would be kitting out and staffing the shops. The commercial success of the venture would depend on whether they could make sufficient extra sales to compensate them for the margin they had lost by buying-in rather than making their own sandwiches. Sales increased quite quickly by 18 per cent, but they needed about 23 per cent to make it viable and they decided to stop the trial after three months. It was a real shame, but I was very grateful for the opportunity, and it would have been amazing if it had worked.

Luckily, we also had a lot of other new business in the pipeline and had started supplying more and more other caterers. Having a full pipeline of potential new business was always very important to me, acting as a form of comfort blanket, and knowing that, as long as there was other business out there that we had a good chance of winning, we wouldn't be quite so vulnerable to our existing clients. We were by now supplying most of the biggest catering companies and the story had been the same with all of them: that as soon as we started with one unit, then word would spread to other units run by the same caterer and they would ask us to go and see them. It was a great feeling and we knew that if we could get our sandwiches in front of someone, then there was a very good chance that they would start buying from us.

CHAPTER 11

The Golden Years

By 2004 we were getting some really good feed-back from our clients, and even our suppliers would report back to us the positive comments they'd heard about us when dealing with our competitors. We never wanted to become complacent or arrogant, but we did by this stage feel we were the best in the country at what we did, and that was an incredible feeling. It was important this message was communicated throughout the company and that everyone took pride in what they did as a result. I very much managed the business by walking around, and being a nuisance and interrupting people to have a chat and see how they were getting on. We realised that we needed a bit more of a structure for our communication and that everyone loved talking about their role and what could be done to improve it, but it was all a bit too random. We then introduced quarterly reviews for office staff and kitchen managers and annual reviews for the rest of the staff. This was certainly not an appraisal as that word has too much of a negative connotation of being judged, and it was important that this initiative was seen by everyone to be a positive thing, and to be looked forward to rather than dreaded. We refined the questions as we progressed, trying as in all things, to keep it as simple as possible with the result that, having started with a form with ten sections to fill in, we eventually refined it down to just five. The idea was that we would give the forms out for the staff to fill in themselves, and we would then sit down and go through them together. A big part of our thinking was also that, regardless of the role, there is no one in a better position to tell you how a job can be improved than the person doing it. The five questions we ended up with for the office staff and managers were:

What do you most enjoy about your job?

What do you least enjoy about your job?

What have you achieved in the last three months?

What do you hope to achieve in the next three months?

What can we do to help you?

The first two questions are really asking what they are good at and not so good at, and we found we received much more honest answers to this question than by asking directly. People are understandably reluctant to write down something they're not good at, but might well express what they least enjoy. And we are generally not so good at the things we don't enjoy. The other great benefit was that it gave everyone an opportunity to express something they may not be happy about, but hadn't bothered to raise before. The other questions are designed to get people to take stock, think about their role, and what they are doing in it, and what they can do to improve it.

The main benefit, however, was that it gave us an opportunity to sit down one to one, and that was worth its weight in gold. Everyone likes to be listened to, and almost everyone likes to have the opportunity to talk about themselves, but how often do either of those two things ever happen? Very rarely. It's flattering to be asked what one's opinion is about something – almost anything – and this provided a great framework for just that. Seham spoke to the kitchen managers and I spoke to the office staff, and it also provided us with an opportunity to talk about our plans for the company, and how important their role was, and why we needed as a company to constantly push forward and avoid standing still. At the same time, we also started a kitchen committee which Seham and I met with once a month made up of volunteers from different parts of the kitchen to represent the views of the kitchen as a whole, both for improvements they thought they could make to our production efficiency, as well for as any improvements we could make to their working conditions. Typical suggestions would be to have one less person on a certain production line, or to pre-mix some ingredients rather than add them individually on the line, through to providing more flexi-time for some staff, or buying new toasting machines for the staff room (however accurate we tried to be with our production numbers, we would inevitably make too many sandwiches every day and the 'extras' would be put in a fridge in the staff room from which everyone would help themselves for lunch).

In addition to this Seham would regularly gather all the kitchen staff and update them with any news, particularly about any new business that was about to start. Occasionally I would join her and say a few words, particularly if we had had a record month, always telling them what a great job they were doing and how important their work was to the success of the company. I would repeat this message at our annual barbecue in the summer, which was always a brilliant event. We turned our loading bay into a dance floor, hired a PA system for our resident salesman/dj David Fat-Boy-Singh, a few of our kitchen managers prepared much of the food, and our transport manager Kamel and I would man the barbecue. Because of working in different shifts, it was the one occasion during the year when the whole company would get together, and we had a blast. We had twenty-eight different nationalities working for us and they would all be dressed up for the party and danced their socks off – an incredible sight.

Rowan was by now married and pregnant and had decided she wanted to stay at home after the baby was born, so it was sadly time to find someone new. I had become used to having someone nannying me, and loved it as I was always thinking of new ideas but had been very bad at seeing them through. With Rowan and Seham working closely together we could speedily implement the necessary actions and, best of all, once I had talked to them about something I didn't have to think about it any more, I knew it would be done. I had been very lucky with Rowan and was very fussy about her replacement. This began to drive her mad as she had arranged about fifteen different interviews and I hadn't wanted to employ any of them. It was a critical role for me; we would be sharing an office and I couldn't risk the wrong person, and would much rather have no one for a while if it came to it. Eventually just as I was rushing out to a meeting a girl came in for an initial interview with Rowan, I had a quick two-minute chat with her on my way out and when I returned later told Rowan that I thought she was the right one. She agreed and Sarah took over and did a great job for the next five years.

Looking back over the twenty-three years I ran Daily Bread, I would say that these were the golden years. I never stopped worrying, and we always had to deal with issues or threats to the business, but in general things couldn't have been better. We were expanding at over 20 per cent a year, we were getting really good feedback from clients and, best of all, we had a great team in place doing a fantastic job and enjoying working with each other. I had always thought that real success would be when the company became self-propelled – in other words would have its own forward momentum and wouldn't need me to drive it, and we were pretty much at that stage. I had become so good at giving responsibility to others that I was beginning to make myself redundant. At first it was a little scary. For the first time I didn't know every client, or every detail of what was going on; however, on the other side it was incredibly liberating, and felt great.

Seham had been a tower of strength over the previous few years. I know we would not have survived without her and her relentless and total commitment to the cause, and I was keen to show my appreciation. It was time to celebrate her tenth anniversary at Daily Bread and Harriet and I took her out to dinner in the River Room at the Savoy. I had asked Harriet earlier to remind me towards the end of dinner to give Seham a birthday card and make it look as if I had forgotten about it. After an excellent dinner the time duly came and I fished around and found the card and gave it to Seham. She opened it and burst into tears, sitting sobbing as she stared at us in shock. Inside was a cheque for £250,000.

Many of the things I'd learnt initially in the Anthony Robbins book were re-enforced by the speakers at our ACE meetings and one that stood out for me was that 10 per cent of life is what happens to you, and 90 per cent is how you respond to it. I have used this a lot over the years and teaching myself to choose my response has become more and more of a habit. I was approaching fifty and that was hard to get my head round. Being in your forties is OK, but fifty was *old* and there was no getting away from it. I still felt about thirty-five and so fifty was unthinkable. Then I decided to flip the whole thing on its head and made up my mind that there was nothing I could do about it and I would not only celebrate being fifty, but would do something every month of my fiftieth year to celebrate it. Suddenly it became something to look forward to.

The ultimate example of choosing one's response was to be a year later when my father suddenly died. He was eighty years old, but had been very fit, playing tennis and golf every week, then suddenly caught pneumonia and within two weeks that was that. It was a devastating time, but I have forced myself since then to celebrate his life and how lucky we were to have him for as long as we did, and to reflect on how much he had enjoyed life, rather than focus on the fact that he's not with us any more. I miss him every day, but insist on keeping my thoughts positive. I was also really pleased that he had lived to see Daily Bread working well, and witness my family and me enjoying the fruits of its success.

We were by now turning over more than £9m and I was beginning to really enjoy our success. I had never striven to make money for the spending of it, just the security and freedom it would give, and that was turning out to be every bit as precious as I always thought it would be. We did, however, take 20 friends to a great hotel in Marrakesh owned by Richard Branson's sister and had an amazing few days there as part of the celebrations for my 50th. Harriet and I had arrived the day before everyone else descended and Richard and his parents were staying. As nice, normal and charming a family as one will meet, and very good at taking the piss out of each other – always a good sign.

By 2005 we were up to over £11m turnover and were really flying. We had had the same team in place for some time now and everyone was still making small adjustments to improve their department's roles. James had left to set up his own business and had remained as a non-exec and Terry had taken over all the accounting function. Terry was as organised as I was chaotic and I had come to realise how important it is that you surround yourself with people who complement you. We kept the reporting as simple as we could and the only figures I was interested in were the key ones: turnover, food, packaging, transport and direct labour. If any of these looked too high, or low, I could then drill down into the detail, and the rest of our costs were fixed and so there wasn't much we could do about them. Direct labour was easy to calculate, and the kitchen knew every day what the labour cost per sandwich had been for that day's production. We would do a stock-take every weekend and I would have our food cost figures by the Monday afternoon, and so we knew exactly how we were doing and if any of our costs needed looking into. Our main cost, food, would seldom vary by more than 1 per cent as a percentage of turnover. If it did, then we would immediately investigate, whether it was up or down. If it was up it would be costing us and we would be losing margin. If it was down, then there was a chance we were under-filling our sandwiches, and that would have to be addressed. I personally signed off all invoices before they were paid which kept me fully in the loop on all our expenditure and was a great way of keeping everyone on their toes, and I never hesitated to query anything I didn't understand, however small. Otherwise we had monthly management accounts which Terry had managed to get down to producing by the 9th or 10th of the following month. The other monthly figures I was interested in was a chart showing all our top clients and what their turnover was as a percentage of our total turnover. We had by now managed to maintain most of our business with our largest client, but they had dropped from over 30 per cent to just under 20 per cent of our turnover as we found new business elsewhere, and so we were moving in the right direction.

If a potential client ever asked me at this time what was the difference between our competitors and us, my immediate response would be 'culture'. We had inevitably employed some people over the years that had worked for other sandwich manufacturers and they would without fail comment on how differently they were treated by us and how different our operation was compared with what they were used to. It really had become like joining a family and the key difference and advantage it gave us was that everyone cared about what they were doing, and cared about the company. Almost every visitor commented on the atmosphere, from the way someone had asked if they could help them when they first arrived outside our units, to the buzz in the office and kitchen. Of course, to us it was normal, and it was easy to forget that maybe other companies operated in a different way. Happy staff worked better than unhappy staff, and so it seemed totally obvious to us to do all we could to keep it that way. At the risk of being repetitive, this was all to do with Seham's stewardship, and her masterly combination of strict discipline and genuine caring. In total contrast to a few years previously, I now positively looked forward to coming into work. Another invaluable by-product of this approach was that we always had people wanting to join us, and never had to use an agency to find new kitchen staff. I would often come in to work and find a queue of people waiting outside our unit to see if we had any vacancies.

The Royal Warrant Holders Association had kindly asked me to join their council a couple of years before, and this was one club I had been very happy to join. A new Royal Charter for the Association had now been drawn up, and the Queen had invited the council to Buckingham Palace to celebrate this. For the first time I would drive through the main gates rather than the tradesmen's entrance, and that was quite a different experience. We were individually introduced to the Queen, and then there were a couple of short speeches. Shortly afterwards the Queen began to circulate amongst the room and I found myself talking to her for a couple of minutes about Daily Bread. The Queen was incredibly charismatic and totally engaging and it was an amazingly special and surreal moment. As I drove home that evening, I couldn't help but reflect on the extraordinary journey that had taken me from wandering round offices selling sandwiches from a basket, to explaining my business to our Sovereign (who, incidentally, took a lot more interest in it than the average dinner party guest!).

I was still interested in how we might progress as a business and read another good book that I found interesting. It is called *The Goal* by Eliyahu Goldratt and is a business book, but written as a (bad) novel about a guy trying to save the steel plant he runs from going bust. The central message is to look at everything you are doing and decide if it is taking you towards, or away from, your goal. It may sound very simple, but it is quite an interesting test. I loathe wasting time, and so would use this as a way of keeping myself in check. The other main message is to look for the bottleneck in your business. What is the one main thing that is stopping your business from growing? In a manufacturing business this could be storage for components, lack of manufacturing space, lack of sales, inability to deliver, or a host of other things. By identifying and focusing on the one main issue that is getting in the way of progress, you can then set to work trying to deal with it.

CHAPTER 12

Heading for the Exit

By 2006 we were still going at full speed ahead and had reached a turnover of £12m. David had done an excellent job in getting new sales in and had helped us expand into hospitals and universities. I would never have thought of universities being our market, but it's amazing how much money students seem to have, and they were prepared to pay for a good sandwich. We still had one main competitor, but then a manufacturer that had specialised in cheap and cheerful sandwiches in North London went bust and a firm I'd heard of, Brambles from Middlesbrough, bought their premises. This was irritating as the previous company hadn't been a threat at all, but Brambles made better quality sandwiches and had grown rapidly in the North of England and Midlands. If we were a little put out by these guys being almost gifted a free sandwich factory in the South, it was nothing compared to what Food Partners thought, as they occupied an almost identical place in the market and Brambles would pose a direct threat to their business. We had widened our client base, but had still stuck to just being a premium supplier, whereas they both covered all the bases and had premium, medium and cheap ranges to appeal to every market. Brambles would try and enter our market by undercutting us on price, with the odd success, but we continued to expand. However, our weakness was becoming increasingly that the other two manufacturers had national distribution and we only went as far north as East Midlands airport. There were quite a few large companies, such as Lloyds Bank, who would want the same supplier throughout the country, so that they could offer a consistent level of catering to all their staff, and we couldn't offer that. We still stuck to doing what we could really well, and liked ideally to be within two hours of any client as this would enable us to offer emergency deliveries.

I was once again looking at what the future held, and the idea began to form that we might open a second kitchen in the Midlands. This way we could maintain our model and simply replicate it. We still did everything exactly as we had while we were at Union Court and, ridiculously, were still putting on labels by hand as that was the only way we could maintain our service of offering each client their own prices on the labels. It wasn't easy, but it worked, and so our reasoning was – why risk changing it and becoming more like every other manufacturer? We had looked into every way we could think of to automate this part of our process, but there was nothing we could do without making them earlier and have an earlier order cut-off time, and we weren't prepared to do that. We had senior staff who would be prepared to re-locate and so this remained a possibility, but our concern was the added expense of running a separate production base, and also, if our culture was so important, how easily might we be able to re-create that in the Midlands. We were doing great business in the South, and there was no reason why we shouldn't in the Midlands and the North, but it was a matter of getting our sandwiches there.

Another thing had happened over the past year or so as well, and that was that I noticed myself being a little less engaged. We had a terrific team in place and they were running all the day-to-day, but it had been a long slog to get where we were and my fire had begun to burn a little less brightly. I started wondering if we might join forces with a larger company which could enable me to take a bit of money off the table and continue running it, but with some additional support. It also still interested me how well we were doing with only David devoted to selling, and a lot of his time was spent looking after business he had introduced, and so the question remained as to how well we might do and how quickly we could possibly expand if we had a bigger facility and a full sales team. I had pretty much lost faith in my ability to hire and motivate a sales director, and we had grown at a very good rate anyway, but if we could link up with a company with a built-in sales team, and national distribution, it could be a powerful combination. I discussed this with James and Terry and Seham and we all agreed that we should see what was out there. Since my aborted attempt at selling in 2002, I had given share options amounting to a total of 5 per cent of the company to Seham, Kamel, Terry and David. This would make a very tax efficient way for them to be rewarded if we ever sold the company as they would only pay 10 per cent tax due to taper relief on capital gains for small businesses. The chairman of our ACE group introduced me to a few companies that specialised in buying and selling companies and I decided to go with one called Cavendish. I had no idea what potential buyers might be out there, but thought there might be a food company that was interested in adding our brand to their operation, and even possibly a European company looking to expand into the UK.

One of the options Cavendish came up with was a private equity company called Inflexion. Charles Thompson was the director leading this project and was full of enthusiasm for what we could achieve together; however, his fellow directors wanted to concentrate on the technology sector and so didn't warm to the idea. I had got on very well with

Charles and he rang me up one day and told me he had just met my future chairman and that he would be perfect for me. Peter McPhillips is a straight-talking Liverpudlian who had run Uniq, a £400m-turnover company specialising in the dairy sector, but also incorporating quite a sizeable sandwich business. We got on immediately and had several meetings together, agreeing that if I didn't find a buyer during this exercise, then it would be fun to work together.

Cavendish thought they should check out our competitors and got in touch with Food Partners, and quite soon they were the most interested party. I had dinner with their managing director and the chairman of the holding company that owned them, and the fit was obvious. They had three production facilities and a distribution depot that gave them national coverage and 130 vans instead our 12. We would be a neat brand for them to add to their operation, and of course they would be removing a competitor. They also loathed Brambles as they had been taking more and more business from them, and they often talked about how our companies together would be able to clean up and completely side-line them. By this stage I had decided that if they were the buyer, then I would have to sell my entire holding as I couldn't see myself continuing with a minority stake, and I don't think they would have been interested in buying less than a controlling stake. I was cautious going into negotiations with them, because during the course of any due diligence exercise, you are very quickly stripped naked and I wasn't comfortable with them having access to all our figures, top clients and so on. They were very enthusiastic, and quickly put a very attractive offer on the table. I'd heard too many terrible stories of people accepting shares in the purchasing company instead of cash for their businesses and so I made it clear that any offer would have to be a cash offer. I was also reluctant to have too much of an earn-out based on future profits as, again, once one loses control the company might be run in a different way, different overheads could be apportioned to it as part of the group, and I wouldn't be able to do anything. I also made it clear that if we were going to do anything, then I would want it done quickly as the whole process would inevitably be quite a distraction, and I knew it was essential I didn't take my eye off the ball during the process – we mustn't be weakened in anyway if negotiations broke down.

Once negotiations had progressed to a serious level and it really looked like it might happen, I told the rest of the senior staff. I obviously hadn't wanted to alarm them unnecessarily if it had come to nothing. Everyone understood the rationale, and the main point was that this move would help us grow by removing the main obstacle to our growth, which was national distribution. I had been very nervous about Food Partners coming to see our kitchens and how we worked, as we had been very low-key and private up until that point, but it then occurred to me that they could see how we did what we did, but they wouldn't be able to copy it because they didn't have our staff or culture, and so I stopped worrying. As I spent more time discussing our two businesses with their senior directors I was fascinated to find that none of them apart from their transport director were really operators. Their understanding of their business was very much from an accountant's viewpoint, and I didn't feel they had a proper grasp on how it really ran. I guess this made sense as they had built the business through acquisition, rather than building it up themselves. We had started negotiations in September and by mid-November we were as good as there. There had been a few robust discussions as was to be expected during the negotiations, but I was in the great position of not having to sell the business, and we were still doing really well, and so

I didn't have to concede on any significant points. The other advantage I had was that I wasn't dying to get my hands on some cash so I could go on a spending spree. I'd heard of people selling their businesses getting compromised by having mentally started spending some of the money they thought was coming to them in advance of the deal being concluded. They then ended up being very weak negotiators as they became increasingly desperate for the deal to go through. By the end of November we were days from signing, when communications went quiet. It's interesting how these sorts of discussion have an energy and vibe to them, and suddenly it had changed. There were still promises that everything was on track and discussions amongst advisors continued, but I instinctively knew it had changed and felt in my bones that it wouldn't happen at all if it wasn't completed by Christmas.

By the beginning of January negotiations ground to a halt. They were still interested in principle, but had just taken on the contract to supply Starbucks throughout the country and said they were too busy to continue for now. I had wondered how they were going to cope with such a large contract as well as integrate with us, but was still a bit mystified. They had employed PriceWaterhouseCooper to do their due diligence and they had spent weeks poring over our books which must have cost a fortune. Ever since David Mathewson had set up our original systems, and then with James and Terry, we had always kept our bookkeeping very straight forward, and had meticulous records and had never tried doing anything clever, so that I knew that anyone could look at our books at any time and we would have no concerns. PWC complimented Terry on his records and had been very happy with everything they found. I wasn't upset at negotiations breaking down, and had taken a very fatalistic approach to the whole thing, although I was a little irritated that it had cost us a bit of money and a lot of my time. We had always been very aware that negotiations might have fallen down at any time, and had been determined throughout all the discussions to keep driving our business forward, and not to be left weakened in any way.

Three months later Food Partners bought Brambles, and so we returned to having one major competitor that was now even bigger. They must have been talking to us both at the same time, but such is life.

Peter McPhillips joined us at this stage as non-exec chairman. We had reached a size where I wanted some 'grown-up' help deciding what our future strategy should be, and some fresh thinking brought to the table. With him and James I now felt I had some really good brain power to help with this. Otherwise things very quickly returned to normal, and we continued to trade well with turnover increasing up to over £13m for 2007. In the meantime Food Partners had a lot on their plates integrating their new business and also coping with the huge new Starbucks account. They had strangely decided not to keep the managing director of Brambles, who had done an excellent job, and decided they would run both companies themselves. By September they were having a lot of issues trying to service the Starbucks account and the three directors I had dealt with during our negotiations all suddenly departed. This was of course good news to us as it left them in some disarray, and we continued to expand.

CHAPTER 13

The Final Curtain

I was by now working a four-day week and had a wonderful work/life balance. I was able to take time off to watch the children in matches and spend more time with them during the holidays, which I felt made up for some of the time we had been apart when we had lived in France. So everything was great, but a nagging doubt remained: what to do with the business in the longer term. To continue to grow at a similar pace we would have to spread our net further afield and possibly adapt to new markets. There were still lots of opportunities in the travel, education and health sectors, but if we got any really big contracts then space might well become an issue once again and I would be faced with the tough decision of whether to risk another big roll of the dice and invest in a new and larger facility. We would also have to address the old chestnut of beefing up our sales team.

We were taking the family to Australia for Christmas, and then Harriet and I were going on to join some friends in New Zealand. I would be away for five weeks and I decided I would use this time to think about the next stage for Daily Bread. Our options were to carry on as we were, but strengthening our sales team; to open an additional facility in the Midlands; or to sell up to a larger company which could help us fulfil our potential and enable us to become a national wholesale brand. In the last week of our holiday I finally decided on the latter option and to have one more attempt at finding a buyer for

Daily Bread. I discussed this with Peter and James as well as Seham and Terry on my return and we all agreed that it was worth one more try, and if that didn't work, then on we would go by ourselves. It had been a tough decision and quite finely balanced, and I would once again be very fatalistic about the result. We were trading well, still had a lot of potential, and could now afford to lose over 40 per cent of our business and still survive, so a sale was far from essential. On the other side, we had had a very good run for some time and the bad old days still haunted me, and I wasn't sure how well I would handle it if we went into a downturn. It would also be very nice not to have all the responsibility, and I had become increasingly keen to branch out into other businesses and see if I could use my experience to help other entrepreneurs.

A big decision was whether to use Cavendish once again. I was disinclined to as I reckoned we had tried all their contacts already, and Peter introduced me to Stamford Partners, a company that specialised in buying and selling food businesses. It would cost an additional £50k in up-front fees, but I reckoned it was worth the punt. It was now the end of January 2008 and the rules on taper relief were changing at the end of the tax year, 5th April, increasing the tax rate from 10 per cent to 18 per cent. So the time-scale was very clear, and also very tight. A whole new sales memorandum would have to be prepared, buyers found, due diligence completed and the whole thing wrapped up by the end of March. I was advised that it was do-able, but only just, and Stamford leapt into action. I met with a series of potential buyers, including Food Partners, still keen, and an American company called Hain-Celestial. Hain was a billion dollar company that specialised in wholesaling natural and organic food and cosmetic products. They were a major supplier to Wholefoods amongst others in the US and had bought some non-core businesses in the UK from Heinz. These included a large sandwich factory in Luton supplying Marks and Spencer and the Linda McCartney vegetarian ready-meal business. They were keen to expand in the UK. They liked brands, and were also keen to diversify their sandwich sales rather than rely solely on M&S.

I met with their UK Managing Director and immediately liked him. He was completely down to earth and full of enthusiasm for what our two companies could do together, and discussions began in earnest. Once we had agreed a price they asked for exclusivity for a period, which would exclude us from talking to any other buyer. We were happy to give this for a limited period, as any serious buyer would ask for this before spending a fortune with lawyers and accountants carrying out due diligence. We had also made clear the time scale we wanted to work to and they were confident they could fit in with this, subject to their due diligence on us being satisfactory. James and Terry and ABG, our auditors for the last six years, worked endlessly responding to questions from Hain's accountants, Ernst & Young, and at the same time our two lawyers were picking over every detail of the sale and purchase agreement. It was an incredibly hectic and intense time, but very stimulating. I began to see why corporate lawyers are paid so much as these guys never seemed to sleep. Most evenings I would get calls up until 10 or 11pm either from them or from Stamford Partners who were involved in any negotiating. As negotiations progressed Peter and I flew out to New York to meet the Hain senior management team. The Chairman and CEO of Hain was a very charismatic big bear of a man called Irwin Simon. Like the UK MD, he was completely unpretentious and buzzing with enthusiasm. We went to their local Wholefoods store and what most impressed me was not the staggering amount of products they supplied to them, but the way a man cleaning the floor greeted Irwin like a long-lost friend.

I had explained to them exactly what I thought of Daily Bread and our potential, and our need to recruit some good salesmen as I wasn't very good at selling. After I left the room Irwin apparently asked Peter if I was for real. I think Americans are just not used to someone admitting they're not good at something.

Back in the UK Hain had taken on a company based in Switzerland to handle negotiations. This was bad news as Stamford had come across them before and found them very tricky to handle. They warned me that the waters might become a little more turbulent from now on, and they were right. Starting with small details, there seemed to be more and more things they wanted changing from our original agreement, a bit like a small child constantly nagging away until they receive some concession to keep them quiet. I ended up speaking to Irwin about my frustration with this, and he promised to deal with it. By the middle of March we were pretty much on target to complete by the last week in March. All the advisors were now working close to seven days a week and it was all go. We had always tried to set realistic and achievable sales targets and our sales memorandum showing anticipated sales for the next five years was no exception. We ended up with quite a complicated formula for rewarding me if we performed well in excess of these targets, and their Swiss advisors now started homing in on this area and trying change the formula – naturally in their favour. It was the final straw for me, and when Irwin finally returned my call at 12.30am one Sunday night I told him that I was withdrawing from the sale. I really had had enough, and told him that if this is how they, or their advisors, could behave now, it didn't bode well for the future and I wasn't prepared to put up with it. It was a pity after all the work that had been put into making the deal happen, but that was that. He said he remained determined to conclude the deal and promised to look into it and come back to me. The next day Stamford had an email from Hain's advisors apologising for the error and explaining that the change was meant to be in our favour not theirs, and it had been a typo error. We resumed negotiations cautiously, and the battle lines were now very clear – one more adjustment and we were gone.

I was very aware that the whole thing might still trip up, and so had to remain quite sanguine about it as we approached the end of March, partly as a defence mechanism, and partly because that seemed the most practical way to approach the whole thing. We were continuing to trade really well and so I was genuinely reconciled to carrying on as we were if it came to it. Stamford, who had a lot to gain from the sale as their fee was largely success based, were very impressively punchy in leading our negotiations, and also in insisting on the agreed time scale being kept to. I admired them hugely for this, as a lesser company might well have been tempted to concede on more points just to hurry the thing along. Finally, at 8.00pm on 1st April I went to Hain's lawyers' offices next to St Pauls with my lawyer and Nick and Simon from Stamford. It was a very strange atmosphere and we hung around in a meeting room for some time before a mass of documents were produced that I had to sign. Then a bit more awkward hanging around after their lawyer left the room, rather like being in a dentist's waiting-room but without the comfort of an old dog-eared copy of *Country Life* to leaf through. Finally their lawyer re-appeared, came up to me and shook my hand and said, 'Congratulations.' I looked at my lawyer in some sort of stupefied disbelief, looking for reassurance that this was OK. After all, I hadn't even been given a cheque which was how I assumed these things worked. It was after 9pm by now and so a bank transfer couldn't take place. He quickly explained that if their lawyer had said it was finalised, then it was the same as having the money in the bank. I'm not often lost for words, and stood there in a quiet daze.

It was all over.

They had brought in champagne and some food and I was thirsty but didn't want to drink, and hungry but didn't want to eat, and instead simply thanked everyone very much for all their hard work and then walked out into the night. Before I got to my car I paused on the pavement and texted Harriet who was at home in the country. I just wrote 'It's done.'

Two Years Later

So, what did it feel like having sold my business – my creation, my baby, my life's work? It felt great. I felt I had taken it as far as I could, I had fretted and worried and obsessed about it for twenty-three years and knew it was time to pass it on to new hands. I still remained very ambitious for Daily Bread and felt that a larger company, with a built-in sales and marketing department and all the other infrastructure a large company needed, as well as huge spare capacity in their own factory, would help us fulfil our potential. There was no premium sandwich wholesale brand in the UK and I could see the business filling that role on a national scale. I had also reached a level of financial independence that I had always craved, and so the primary aim when setting up the business had been achieved and it felt the right time to move on to doing something else, using my experience to see how I could help others.

One thing I do regret is not being able to be President of the Royal Warrant Holders Association. In 2005 I had been asked by the Association's Council to be President for 2010 (it is an annual appointment). In 2008 the Association then asked me if I would postpone my Presidency until 2012 as it was the Queen's Diamond Jubilee and would be a very significant year for the Association. This was hugely flattering and I agreed. I also thought that I would be entering the end of my earn-out in 2010 and it may have been a good thing not to have the distraction that year (there are about 50 events to attend and speak at during the Presidential year, so quite a commitment). Half way through 2010 it transpired that as I was no longer actively engaged with the business, I no longer officially qualified to be the Grantee of our Warrant and I resigned from the Council. A real shame, and my one regret as it would have been a great honour and I would have enjoyed it – all quite grown-up stuff, but I would have thrown myself at it and was looking forward to breathing a bit of fresh air into what is a gloriously staid and traditional organisation. I should have stuck with 2010 and would have been fine, and what a way to go out, but there we are. A bird in the hand . . .

It is difficult seeing your business run by other people. There are inevitably differences in style, and the dynamics change. However, I know that it was the right thing to do, both for me and for the business itself. A negative I have encountered is that when I was asked what I did for a living I would always reply that I sold sandwiches ('No, what do you *really* do?' 'No that *is* what I do . . . ') and I now have to dream up another answer. I miss that. I miss the people, all of them, and the warmth and camaraderie we enjoyed. As clichéd as it may sound, we really did have a feeling of being part of one big family, and I know I will never work in such an atmosphere again.

My way of handling the aftermath of the sale of the business was to carry on exactly as usual. This may sound dull, but it felt right to me, and besides, I had been pretty much living the life I wanted for the past few years, and so why change it? I told my family and a few close friends, left the proceeds from the sale in the bank, and tried as much as I could to keep my head down. (I did, however, get quite a bit of flak for admitting that we had, at last, bought a new dishwasher at home that actually worked properly!) What was different was that I didn't have such a huge burden of responsibility on my shoulders any more. I was contracted to work two days a week for the following two years and, despite only being paid for the two days, I continued to work four days a week as that's what felt most comfortable. I liked the new owners and was keen to help them as much as I could to continue with the company's progress. This went really well for the first six months, with everything on target and good progress being made. Then came September 2008 and the financial world started falling apart and the trickle-down effect of companies cutting back on all expenditure, including catering, started. This made business much harder and a new price competitiveness entered the market, but we had had tough times before, and I knew we could manage that.

What I found most difficult, however, was trying to handle a new beast altogether, and that was called an HR department. Whoever came up with an expression such as 'Human Resources'? There's something shockingly Orwellian about it – and this turned out to be in actions as well as words. These guys ran the business, mainly through their legal knowledge and the constant threat that if X or Y wasn't done the company might get sued for any number of absurd reasons. 'What was our bullying and harassment training policy? We didn't have one? Well, what would our defence be if we were ever accused of it?' 'Well, we have the happiest staff you'll ever come across and not one person has accused us of such a thing in 23 years.' 'Still, you'd have no defence if a charge was pressed . . .' and so on. It drove me mad, and I couldn't bear to see my office invaded by such time-wasting and inefficient bureaucracy. It was then pointed out to me that, actually, it wasn't my office any more.

I couldn't blame our parent company in the US for backing

the HR department, as they had an understandable fear of any possible litigation. I also realised after a year or so that I was distinctly unhappy not being in control. I was too used to it and, try as I might, I wasn't good at sitting on the sidelines; Peter McPhillips, my Chairman from Daily Bread, who had by now become Chairman of our parent company, Hain Europe, regularly had to remind me that you can't sell your house and then dictate to the new owners what colour they should paint the walls. We agreed that I should be paid a monthly retainer and move to a non-exec role for the remainder of my two-year contract. I was out.

I still care hugely about Daily Bread. I continue to worry about it, and probably always will.

Running Daily Bread was an amazing experience that I still can't fully take in. It very nearly got the better of me, and then ended up giving me more satisfaction, fulfilment and reward than I could ever have dreamt of. I have been exceptionally fortunate, and if this book serves to help motivate, inspire or teach something to even one person, then its job is done.

I suppose the main message I hope to get across is that *anyone* can have a degree of success in business, provided they have some common sense and drive and are prepared to throw themselves wholeheartedly at it. I don't think there are many short-cuts and I guess most people's hopes are that they can find one – I certainly idled away many an hour when I was in my twenties dreaming of finding some quick-fix solution to becoming rich – something I failed dismally at, and hence the need to start buttering bread aged thirty-one . . .

One of the big decisions in life revolves around one's suitability to working for oneself or for others. There is no right or wrong to this – everyone is different and while some relish having their own enterprise, others are much happier in a more structured environment and being part of a bigger setup. I was asked recently whether entrepreneurs are born or made. After some thought, my conclusion was that they are born. Why? Because I think you have to be naturally rebellious and questioning to become an entrepreneur, and happy to endlessly challenge the status quo. You also need to be something of a risk taker and, as mentioned above, you need an innate drive attached to a good dose of common sense and both these characteristics are part of your DNA and can't be taught. Add a little confidence, and off you go.

Luckily, what you don't need is to be hugely academic. It's not a coincidence that so many well-known entrepreneurs have few academic qualifications; after all, if you leave Oxford with a double first you are more than likely to be besieged by irresistible offers from top City companies and set on a structured career path before you can say 'million pound bonus'. There is a wonderful story of Hughie Hodgkinson, the headmaster of my own fine academic institution, Milton Abbey (a public school well known for its lack of academic excellence, but very good at building confidence and en-couraging individuality), going to Eton many years ago to speak to the boys in their last year. They were on the edge of their seats as he praised them and their institution, telling them that they were at the finest school in the country, with unrivalled facilities and tutors and how there was no doubt they were set for great things. He had them in the palm of his hand. At the end he paused and asked them to just reflect on one thing, however: 'What you will feel like when you are working for my boys – because you will be.'

You could argue that lack of academic qualifications almost forces some people to set up their own enterprises, and I'm sure that is often the case, but I think there is something deeper ingrained – the born bit – that drives most entrepreneurs.

Setting up my own business I never thought of myself in such exotic terms as an entrepreneur – I just wanted to work for myself and run my own business, and be directly rewarded for my endeavours. I think there is beginning to be a danger that the very word 'entrepreneur' has had a certain glamour attached to it thanks to TV programmes (and just look at the 'stars' on those shows for proof of my above theory . . .). The word 'entrepreneur' comes to equal success and making lots of money. Entrepreneur . . . Ferrari. The problem is that there is that little awkward bit in between the two that needs to be addressed.

It's also worth pointing out that not everyone setting up their own business does it to make money. Many do it for the lifestyle it can give them and the ability to march to their own tune, and as long as there is sufficient money coming in to survive, then they are happy. I have a lot of respect for that position, and am in a way quite jealous of it and the contentment it implies, but my drive was always centred around trying to make money, so that I could hopefully one day have the independence and freedom I so craved. I'm often amazed when I hear successful entrepreneurs say they didn't set out to make money and that it has been a pleasant by-product of their efforts, and suspect some of them may confuse their current position (when of course money is no longer their main driver) with their attitude and fiscal determination when they first started.

My advice to any aspiring entrepreneur would be to try and get a job in a leading company in the field you are interested in first. During this time you will learn a huge amount about the industry and how it works. You will find out where supplies or services are bought from, who the big clients are in that industry and how to sell to them, as well as what sort of margins are made. Equally importantly, you will see the good and the bad in how they motivate and discipline their staff, which can be hugely beneficial when it comes to formulating the kind of culture you want to develop when you have your own business. You can also learn from the mistakes they make – so much better at their expense than your own. Every company gets things wrong sometimes, and this must be accepted. What isn't acceptable is not learning from them. During this time you may decide to stick with the company as you like its culture, and feel you have a real possibility to grow with it, maximising your potential and being rewarded accordingly. There is a certain comfort in being part of a larger company with an established infra-structure around you, allowing you to get on with your specific role. You also benefit from the credibility that that company will have established in its field, allowing you to be taken more seriously when making sales calls for instance. If, however, you feel you can do a better job, and are not really listened to, or the ladder to the top looks too long for your liking, then you will have learnt some great lessons and it becomes a matter of putting them into practice.

Some people think it's brave setting up your own business, and I can see what they mean. However, I think it's quite brave working for others. At least you know when you're going to be sacked when you work for yourself – I always had that lurking fear when I worked for other companies that they would realise how little they needed me when I went on holiday, which always added a small frisson of discomfort to my return . . .

So, how to best summarise everything I feel I have learnt over the twenty-three roller-coaster years spent running my own business? The roller-coaster bit is important, as it is in the tough times that you learn the most. Many of the points below have been covered already in the context of my Daily Bread story, but I thought it worth giving them a brief recap. It is important to mention that what follows are the lessons that I've learnt, and that have worked for me. I would never say they are necessarily the right or the correct or the only way; they are simply views I have developed as the result of my own experiences, as well as from being an endlessly curious witness to how other people respond to challenges in their lives.

SIZE MATTERS

It's important to be clear on your motivation when setting up a business. If it is primarily to make money, rather than a lifestyle business, then how big can it ever potentially be? Does the idea have scale, and if it does, then what is the approximate size of the prize – how big could it possibly become? Have a clear picture in your mind of how you hope the business will develop, as well as the type of people you imagine working with before setting forth. Critically, where is the break-even point? You can break-even forever, but can only lose money for a very finite period of time. This, together with an accurate cash-flow forecast, will also determine the amount of cash you will need before starting your venture.

When setting up a business, try not to use your own name as the business name. The danger is that as time goes on and the company develops, you may become too associated with it, and people will want to talk only to the engineer, and not the oily rag. By giving it a different name, you also have a better chance of giving the impression that the company is bigger than it actually is, which can be an advantage, particularly at the beginning. The main benefit, though, is when you come to passing on the company to your management, or selling it; if your main clients, or potential purchasers, associate your name too closely with the company, they may well be nervous if you will no longer be working for it.

KISS (keep it simple, stupid)

This is the big one, and applies to all aspects of life, and particularly in business. Constantly look to see how you can simplify things. Challenge everything you and your business does, all the time, and see if there is an easier or quicker way of doing it. Also encourage all your staff to do the same. The natural caveat is of course that quality/service must NEVER suffer as a result.

Some people think life is basically simple. And in a way it should be, but I don't think it is. It naturally becomes quite complicated quite quickly, and instead you have to really work at sticking to the important stuff and letting the rest go. Left to its own devices endless bits creep in around the edges, and so it pays to regularly assess what you are doing and seeing if it can be simplified in any way.

Choose your battles – you can't fight on every front at the same time.

Try not to discuss contentious issues or points of irritation in the heat of the moment; much better with a cool head when you can have a much more balanced and measured discussion – and to a generally more receptive audience. When upset by someone or something, try sleeping on it. It's amazing how often things don't matter so much the next day.

Look for the bottleneck in your business and make that your primary focus – what is the one main area that is holding back the progress of the rest of the company?

If you have a big challenge, then break it down to bite-sized chunks and tackle it one stage at a time. The whole picture can sometimes look intimidating, and it's important to work your way through it in a methodical manner. Everything can be overcome with enough persistence and hard work. Don't forget that if there were no problems, then you wouldn't have a job. You are paid to sort them out. After all, if your business was that easy, then all your competitors would also be doing an excellent job and your point of difference would be gone.

Thinking of which . . .

DON'T BE AVERAGE

If you are average, it is hard to see why anyone would want to use your product or service. There need to be at least three killer reasons why a potential client would want to use you. Work out what your 'elevator pitch' is (the time it takes for the lift to travel a few floors before your audience gets out) and constantly look to refine it. You also have to passionately believe it – if you don't, why should anyone else?

The primary reasons someone will use your company will be convenience, speed of delivery, price, quality and service. One of these will be the dominant feature, and then you will need to work on the subtext clarifying exactly what the credentials are that make your company so outstanding in that area.

CASH COUNTS

Businesses don't go bust because they are losing money, they go bust because they run out of cash (many businesses lose money for years before turning a profit, which is fine as long as they are well funded and have sufficient cash to see them through).

Cash-flow is the most critical element of any company, and developing an accurate cash-flow forecast is perhaps the most valuable contribution your accountant can make. Cash must be controlled with a vengeance – count every penny and challenge every expense, regardless of how well you are doing. Too many companies allow themselves to get fat and happy and into bad habits when things go well, and get a rude shock when their business suffers a down-turn. There is also little point struggling to get money coming through the front door, if you are allowing it to trickle its way out of the back door. Insist you are paid on time, and don't hesitate to cease supply if a client has started mucking about and making excuses to pay you late – it generally means they are either very badly managed, in which case a sharp warning will probably sort them out, or they are in trouble, in which case you want nothing to do with them. If you are worried about a client's credit worthiness, then either don't deal with them, or severely reduce the credit you are prepared to give them. It is sometimes better to swallow a small loss than allowing a debt to escalate and, above all, you cannot allow yourself to become vulnerable to them.

Try and build up cash reserves in the business for protection against a rainy day. This also serves as a buffer between you and the need for a bank loan. It may well be necessary to take out a bank loan at some point, in which case try and avoid giving a personal guarantee if at all possible (and you may well not be able to avoid it, particularly in the early days when there aren't likely to be many assets in your company to borrow against). Make sure the agreed repayment plan is achievable, and that there is no penalty for paying it off early – you don't want to be vulnerable to a bank manager for any longer than is absolutely necessary.

Make sure you are buying competitively, but treat your suppliers with as much respect as your clients, always pay on time and treat them as you would like your clients to treat you. You all need each other.

WATCH THE BOTTOM LINE

'Turnover is vanity, profit is sanity' may be a very overworked cliché, but it's also very true.

Remember why you started your business, and don't be seduced by large sales opportunities if you're not going to make any money out of them. *Don't be afraid to say no.* It sounds obvious, but it is one of the biggest single mistakes many businesses make, being intoxicated by the lure of large volume, thinking the numbers are so big that they *must* make something out of it, and then finding that the supposed cost savings and economies of scale aren't what they thought, and they are in fact making a loss on the business. It is also worth keeping a constant eye on the smaller bits of business that you did in the early days and see if they are still justified and are making any money, or are they clogging up the system and putting a strain on your logistics and are they now, to put it simply, more trouble than they're worth?

Be clear what margins you want to work to and stick to them. If you offer a volume-related discount, then make it consistent and transparent to all your clients. The danger of offering a special deal to one large client is that if a manager from that company leaves them to join a rival they will expect you to offer them the same deal.

Thinking of large clients, try and avoid any one client accounting for more than 25 per cent of your business. Any more than this and you will be too vulnerable and end up dancing to their tune and not yours. If they should threaten to withdraw all their business if you don't give them an additional 5 per cent discount it may well be tempting to accede. The problem is that this will most likely become an annual discussion. The cheaper your price becomes, the more they will be encouraged to use you, making them an even larger client and so on, until you are totally at their beck and call, and making almost no margin at all – the last reason you wanted to set up your own business in the first place. If one client does start becoming a large percentage of your business, then let it act as a spur to push you to find alternative additional business in order to dilute them.

KEEP POSITIVE

This is often easier said than done, and I think it's a fascinating subject. You need to be of a positive disposition to even think of setting up your own business. I have listened over the years to countless business coaches/speakers and the consistent central message from almost all of them is to get positive, be positive, stay positive. It is of course essential, and acts as a great motivator and driver both for you and for anyone working with you.

It must, however, be tempered by a sense of realism, and a good dose of common sense. Some of the most dangerous businessmen I have come across have been relentlessly positive, and while optimism is great, blind optimism can be lethal. The problem is that they always *know* that their venture is going to be a huge success. They *know* that their new product is going to take the market by storm, and whatever money they need to invest in it is easily justified by this guaranteed success. They never stop to think, 'What if . . . ?' Is the product/service really that good? Will that potential huge order really come in, and what do we do if it doesn't? They're travelling so fast they don't see the signs warning of a bumpy road ahead, and would probably ignore them anyway if they happened to glance at them as they rushed past. They are so confident in themselves, that failure is never contemplated and potential problems are ignored. This attitude can be very dangerous, and is more often than not combined with an unshakeable belief that as long as enough sales are made eventually all will be well, while forgetting that there may be considerable extra expense in servicing those sales – let alone whether there is sufficient capacity in the factory/office. The other characteristic shared by such people is almost always an inability to listen or take advice – about which more later.

The key then, is to fully explore the negatives of any project before embarking on it. While this might seem blindingly obvious, it is frequently the case that people's enthusiasm gets the better of them and the downside is either ignored or glossed over.

So, having seen what's great about some new initiative, then look at what might be bad about it. How much will it cost, can you afford it, will anyone want to buy it, what benefit will it bring, what is the risk, and what is the pay-back? Getting the balance right between unquestioning optimism and a more measured pragmatic approach is difficult, and best achieved as you progress by employing people who complement each other's characters (as well as your own).

It is easy, as the boss, to care *too* much about your business and all the hard work that has gone into it, and to get to a point where any criticism or problems are exaggerated in your mind to the point where you can think of little else (I put my hands up here) – to become so obsessed by an issue that if you are told five good things have happened and one slightly bad, that you focus almost entirely on the bad thing.

You can, however, teach yourself to be in a more positive state of mind, and this is where the power of NLP (Neuro Linguistic Programming) comes in – think of it as your brain being the most incredible computer, but it comes with no operating instructions. NLP is a method of bringing some control to how it works, and while I don't know that much about it, and it's many years since I've read any books dealing directly with it (my knowledge coming from Anthony Robbins books, as well as hearing many motivational speakers discussing it over the years), I still find what I learnt useful. Incidentally, I personally find anything, or anybody, that goes to extremes off-putting and irritating, and NLP is no different, so best taken in small doses and sometimes with a pinch of salt.

During the tough times I used to sometimes worry too much about my business, and I knew this was having a negative effect on how I was running the company and it was de-motivating for both myself and my colleagues. This is what I learnt: Recognise when you are in a negative mood and clarify in your own mind what it is that is concerning you. Try and visualise it and then, as if pulling an aerial out of the back of a TV, scramble the image and make it fuzzy. Then force yourself to think of something, anything, positive. It could be as simple as what you're having for dinner that night, a film you want to see, holiday to look forward to, or whatever. Almost immediately you should feel more cheerful and energised, and you will then be in a much better position to handle whatever it is that has been concerning you. I read somewhere that it takes twenty days to form a habit and recognising when you are in a negative mood, and deciding to do something about it, is an amazing habit to get into.

I find the science of neurology fascinating, and the fact that we can change the way our minds work had a pretty life-changing effect on me – and without a doubt helped transform the way I ran my business. Having learnt so much, and seen the almost immediate benefits, I became very receptive to any new ideas, and have remained interested in learning more ever since. The way I look at it is simple: If someone can show me how to get a 2 per cent improvement in a business's performance, I'm all ears.

With modern scanning techniques scientists can now see

the effect thought patterns have on the brain, and how for instance serotonin (the 'feel good' hormone) is released by positive thoughts and cortisol (the bad 'stress' brother) is released by negative thinking. Imagine seratonin creating a series of dashes all in a line representing a train of thought. When cortisol is introduced, every other dash moves from horizontal to a vertical position blocking the train of thought, which is why when people are in a 'negative' mood, they find it very difficult to make decisions or think clearly.

Your mood also affects others: I read somewhere that, as a boss, the tone in the office is set for the day by how you behave in the first two minutes after arriving in the morning. It's obviously not a foolproof formula, but it had enough of a ring of truth to it for me to remember it thereafter every day as I was about to walk up the stairs to our office. There had been times in the past when I might walk in slightly distractedly, thinking of something unconnected to work, and I would be taken aside later on and asked what was concerning me. I had no idea anyone would have noticed, and it took me some time to appreciate that others might take their lead from me, and if I appeared (rightly or wrongly) to be worried, then others would worry also, assuming something was wrong with the company. Another big lesson that follows on from this, is that as the boss, you're not allowed to have an 'off' day. You have to be positive and upbeat, even when you feel sick to the pit of your stomach with worry. You have to have a clarity of vision, and lead the way, particularly when things are going badly, and this can be the toughest part of the job.

Another interesting aspect of being positive, which I find really useful, is when having to discipline people. You can say almost anything to people if it is presented in an upbeat way. If you have something difficult to say, keep it short, keep it upbeat, and keep it clear – no grey wishy-washy areas where they are not quite sure where they stand at the end of your chat.

There are two more expressions I like to remind myself of occasionally that can be helpful:

If you think you can, you can, and if you think you can't,
you can't. Either way, you'll prove yourself right.

You go where you are looking.

This is one of the things you are taught as a motorbike rider; if you go round a corner and focus on the tree you are trying to avoid on the apex, you will have a good chance of hitting it. You have to force yourself to look at the end of the corner, to where you want to go. That way all your weight will move accordingly and you will negotiate the corner smoothly. There are always going to be obstacles on your road, and focusing on your end goal will help provide the energy and direction to get through them.

LANGUAGE IS IMPORTANT

One of the biggest lessons I've learnt is the use of language. I can't stand 'business-speak' and all the pseudo language that some people seem to think passes them off as some sort of authority. The brightest (and most successful) people I know have an ability to explain in extremely simple language what their business does, what differentiates them from their competitors, or details of a certain problem they are dealing with. Conversely, in my experience, less confident people have a tendency to wrap everything up in complicated jargon, particularly if they don't know what they're talking about.

In more general terms, the words one uses daily can have quite an effect. Good examples might be the use of the word 'challenge' rather than 'problem', or 'inconvenient' instead of 'nightmare'. You are dealing with the same issue, but it

has become something you are going to over
some huge negative obstacle to your progre
negative words to become part of your langi
around you.

When someone asks how you are, try and be in the habit
of saying 'Very well' or 'Great', rather than 'OK' or 'Fine' or
'Alright'. It may sound a bit tree-huggy, but just hearing
yourself saying that you feel great can make you feel great,
just as the action of smiling sends a message to the brain that
you are happy. However bad you may have been feeling, you
will immediately feel better just for forcing yourself to sound
more positive. And besides, don't forget that the definition
of a bore is someone who, when you ask them how they are,
tells you.

Another useful tool is physically breaking the pattern. Get
up and move around. Sometimes just taking yourself off for
a brief walk outside, or round the office can add some energy
to a lacklustre day (and we all have them).

LISTEN

The old expression that we are born with one mouth and two
ears, and that they should be used in that proportion, is
never truer than in business. Seek out anyone whose views
you respect, or who has relevant experience, and see what
you can learn from them. Learn everything you can from
other people's experiences. It is quite flattering being asked
for advice, and so most people are more than happy to help.

You have to believe that everything your company does
can be done better and one of the best ways of achieving this
is to listen. Give every single person in your company an
opportunity to put forward any suggestions they may have as
to how to improve things – whether it's regarding their
working environment, or ways the company can be more
efficient. After all, no one is in a better position to comment

...ian the person doing the job day in, day out. Be open to ideas, even if they fly in the face of your own views – there may be something in there worth investigating and trying out.

LEARN FROM MISTAKES

It is essential to be constantly learning and trying to improve one's business, and if you can learn from others' experiences or mistakes, then so much the better.

Thomas Edison failed over 2,000 times in his attempt to invent the electric light bulb. Except he never looked at it as failure. He had simply found 2,000 ways that didn't work. This was progress, he was learning, and we know the eventual result. Mistakes will be made, but learn from them, and make sure they are never repeated.

GRASP THE NETTLE

If you have something awkward to do, a phone call you keep putting off or whatever, just get on and do it. (a) It's almost always not as bad as you think it's going to be and (b) for as long as it's not done, it hangs over you like a cloud. If you have an awkward or important phone call to make, it's also worth standing up when making it, rather than sitting slumped in your chair. This will give you more energy, and ensure you are generally more alert.

In fact, whatever you need to do, just get on and do it as speedily as possible – tomorrow will always be much more busy than you think, so don't leave things for it. A very good rule for time management is to try to touch a piece of paper only once. If you open your mail, deal with each letter as you come to it. You can then file it and move on. This is *much* easier said than done (as my desk would attest), but well worth a stab at.

DON'T LIE

Don't lie, that way you won't have to remember anything . . .

APPRECIATION

Good leadership involves clarity of vision and an unshakeable belief in, and enthusiasm for, your business as well as the people in it. This should prove infectious. Remember that every person's job is essential, and that if it's done badly it will have an impact on the rest of the company. As old fashioned as it may sound, manners are important, and every member of staff, from the cleaners to the directors, should be treated with the same respect (Gordon Ramsay may provide some entertainment with his camp histrionics on TV, but woe betide the manager who believes that is how staff should really be treated . . .). Ask people to do something rather than tell them. Be quick to praise, and try to 'catch people doing things right'. The expression 'Praise in public, damn in private' is worth remembering – no one likes to be publicly humiliated.

Never underestimate the power of appreciation – it is often much more powerful than simply paying someone more. As Mark Twain put it, 'I can go two months on a good compliment.'

BE IN THE ROOM

This is a neat way of trying to help you be more engaged in whatever it is that you are doing. We have all sat in on meetings and drifted off, just as we've sometimes talked to our children about their day at school, and not really been switched on to the conversation. Extraordinarily, my wife frequently accuses me of doing it when she's talking to me about some domestic issue, but I'm sure she's mistaken . . . Anyway, it's worth trying to remember that, 'If you're going to be in the room, then BE in the room' and try and concentrate on the matter in hand. It will be more rewarding for you – and those you are with – and add more intensity to anything you do.

CHOOSE YOUR RESPONSE

10 per cent is what happens to you, and 90 per cent is how you respond to it. Many things will happen to you that are beyond your control. What is in your control, however, is your response to these things, and this will set the tone for those around you. Make this a conscious decision and, naturally, keep it as positive as you can. An excellent question to ask, whenever possible, is, 'What's good about this?' Very often an opportunity can come out of the most dire circumstances.

LEARN TO BREATHE

This is one of the biggest lessons I've learnt and I continue to use it regularly. Whenever you are frustrated, feeling a bit tense, or are generally irritated, try slowly breathing in for five seconds, holding it for five seconds and exhaling for five seconds. Repeat as necessary. This can be done quietly, whether in the middle of a meeting, or the middle of a motorway. It dramatically reduces your heart rate and eases any tension you may feel. It really does work.

SAVE YOUR BREATH

It's really enjoyable trying to help people, and particularly when you feel you can see reasonably clearly what changes might be of value to them. You can only help them, however, if they want to be helped, otherwise you might as well save your breath – it is often astounding how resistant people are to change, even when they are deeply unhappy with the results of their current actions and behaviour. Thinking of which . . .

KEEP ON MOVING

If things don't change, they stay the same. If you keep doing the same thing, why should you ever expect a different outcome? If you keep repeating the same actions or patterns of behaviour, why should you ever get a different result? If you are not happy with any aspect of your business, or how you are running it, then decide what changes you need to make, and get on with it.

This should be a natural process anyway – a business is a living and breathing thing and needs constant sustenance. Like water in a pond, if it's not moving it goes stagnant. For this reason, you can't set a target for a certain profit and then hope to cruise at that altitude once you've reached it, you have to keep moving forwards. Without inertia, a business can quickly go downhill – if you're not going forwards it is too easy to start going backwards, and it's so much harder to turn things around once they have started sliding.

Every business needs a degree of luck or good fortune along the way, and if you do get a break, then run with it and take full advantage of it. Never assume it will last forever. There are times when you have to put your foot to the floor and really capitalise on an opportunity and it's important to recognise these moments.

Once you are employing people, they will want to feel they are on a journey and will want to grow with the company, and keeping things fresh and with a clear path forward is one of your main roles as a leader. This also serves to keep things interesting not just for you, but also your colleagues and of course clients. If you have built up a business it is almost impossible not to worry about it, and this generally serves as a sufficient incentive to keep on pushing forward and to avoid becoming complacent. As they say, only the paranoid survive . . .

Ultimately, you will have built up a valuable business when it is making money and is developing and moving ahead of its own accord, and not relying on your direct input – when it has become self-propelled. This shows you have not just developed good managers, but that you have also given them the autonomy to use their initiative, make decisions, and drive the company forward themselves.

WRITE DOWN YOUR GOALS

The power of the written word is extraordinary, and writing down clearly what your goals and aspirations are can help a lot in formulating what it is that you hope to achieve. An interesting exercise I also did once was filling in a form writing down my goals and sub-goals and all the things I wanted to achieve or change in my life. I then filled in an identical-looking form, but this time pictorially, and using as many different colours as possible. I can't draw to save my life, but the idea was to tune the message into both the left and right sides of the brain. Somehow things are more likely to happen once committed to paper, and the more specific your goals, the sharper the point to aim for, the better.

I did this exercise during the really tough times when the future of the company was in jeopardy (around 1998) and came across it only recently when tidying up my files. I was stunned at the accuracy with which the wish list had been fulfilled, not just in the material areas (nice house, children educated privately) but also in the broader areas such as pursuing hobbies or spending more time with the children – this particularly amazed me as it had been written when there was an almost zero chance of any of these aspirations being realised.

Looking backwards can also be very valuable and, while providing the drive and direction for your business is essential, it's also important to take some time out occasionally to review your progress and give yourself time to reflect. Writing down the things you have achieved in the last three or six months or so, can act as a real boost and help motivate you going forward.

HIRING AND FIRING

Always look to recruit people that will bring complementary skills to the table.

Despite your enthusiasm, there is no way that you can handle every aspect of a business, although you will of course most likely have to muddle your way through somehow in the early days. A bookkeeper/accountant is an obvious starting point. Ideally find someone well qualified but used to a small company environment.

You can divide the world broadly into two halves – the energy givers (sometimes known as radiators) and the energy takers (drains). Energy givers are the sort of people who have an instinctive ability to cheer you up and enthuse you when you're feeling a bit down, and the takers the exact opposite, sapping all your energy and leaving you feeling exhausted after only a brief conversation. It is something that you notice more and more if you switch onto it, and it goes without saying that you want to recruit bright-eyed energetic people that you feel you can spark off.

For senior management, employ the best people you can possibly get as the company grows, and don't worry if they have bigger brains, or salaries, than your own – remember that they are going to be adding value to your business, not theirs.

Be cautious, however, of recruiting from large companies – big isn't necessarily beautiful. As we grew in size we increasingly thought it was time we employed some 'proper professionals' to show us how to do it. This is quite a common error for any growing company; you get to the point where you think you can't carry on somehow 'getting away with it' and need to grow up, and learn how it's really done. Non-execs with good and relevant experience can be very useful, but I would advise against getting in some expensive heavy hitters from large company backgrounds in the hope they will transform your business. They are very often used to a totally different culture where a nice colourful graph at the end of each month suffices to keep their immediate boss happy, but they don't know how to roll up their sleeves and get stuck in, which is almost certainly what you need. Instead, have the courage of your convictions. If it's working, you're doing something right, and it doesn't necessarily need the big fix you think it does. Perhaps the most outstanding example of this was Apple when Steve Jobs brought in some 'professionals' who not only ended up firing him, but also nearly ran the company into the ground.

There are times when you will have to temper your ambitions and head for your horizon a little slower than you would naturally like. Not everyone is as dynamic as you would like them to be, or as committed as you are, and many is the time when you may have to bite your tongue to hide your frustration when things don't happen as fast as you would like. It is essential at these times to take a deeply pragmatic approach and think of the picture as a whole, and respect the fact that while someone might not set the world alight, their overall reliability and honesty have their own value. There are also many reasonably repetitive jobs where these character-istics are much more important than any dynamism.

Beware of troublemakers – the people in your company

who enjoy causing upheaval and unrest, the type who like to snipe away at the water-cooler. It doesn't matter what position they hold in the company, they can cause a lot of damage and you can't afford to tolerate them. They can often work quite subtly, stirring others up, and in my experience the best way to deal with them was the opposite – to speak directly to them and ask what their problem was, see if you could help them, and then make it absolutely clear that you were aware of their behaviour, and it wouldn't be tolerated. These sorts of people tend to be natural bullies, and it's essential they know you're not afraid to stand up to them. No one is indispensable, and sometimes it is unfortunately necessary to remind someone of this. We made a very conscious effort to avoid any office politics, and quickly stamped on any back-biting. You were either in or you were out.

If someone turns out to be not suited to working for your company, then deal with it as soon as possible. This is as much for their sake as yours, and so needn't be handled with great trepidation. Of course it's an unpleasant conversation to have, and of course you would like to put it off for as long as possible, just in case a corner can be turned, but the sooner it is dealt with the better. You know when you have started to lose confidence in someone, and the danger in keeping them on is that their own confidence starts suffering and their performance gets even worse. You can't exactly be cheerful when asking someone to leave, but you can be upbeat and explain as sympathetically as possible that they would be better suited to working in a different environment. I believe everyone is capable of doing really good work, but it's essential that they are in the right environment, and if you can't provide it then it is right for them, for their own sake, to move on.

This is not to be confused with someone going through a

bad patch, and once someone has proved themselves as not only capable but also dedicated, then look after them and take care of them and do whatever it takes to get them back in the saddle – not only will they appreciate it, but it also sends out a very positive message to everyone else: if you want people to genuinely care about your company, then you need to genuinely care about them. A lot of people talk about how important their staff are, but very few really walk the talk and this can give you a real competitive advantage.

Sometimes moving people into different departments, or giving them different roles, can have a major impact on their performance and allow them to shine. Asking someone what part of their job they most enjoy is a very good way of establishing which areas they are most likely to excel in, and was always part of our three-monthly review with our key staff.

Oh, and you *don't* need an HR department! If you can't manage, motivate, discipline and take care of your managers, then you shouldn't be running a company. And if your managers can't manage, motivate, discipline and take care of their staff, then they shouldn't be employed as managers. Make sure you have someone to help check all your contracts and procedures are correct and from whom you can get legal advice, particularly when you need to formally discipline someone, and off you go. It's (almost) as simple as that.

LETTING GO

Once you have developed your company and have the dynamos mentioned above in place, make sure you delegate real responsibility to them and allow them to get on with their jobs. It's very natural, and tempting, to continue to interfere if they are handling a part of the business that you are used to dealing with, but it's essential to let them get on with it once you've given them the necessary initial guidance.

As the business grows, a useful phrase to bear in mind to ensure you are delegating as much as possible is, 'I only do what only I can do.' By backing off from day-to-day duties you will also be in a much better position to make good and clear strategic decisions which are critical to any business's success.

CULTURE IS CRITICAL

If a potential client asked me what the difference was between us and our competitors, I would always reply, 'Culture.' And I meant it. I knew everyone else would bang on about the quality of their products, flexibility of service and so on, and I thought this a nice way of differentiating ourselves. Anyone can produce an amazing sandwich as a sample and deliver it on time for a tasting; however, I would argue that this cannot be done en masse every day unless you have the right culture throughout the company. Creating an environment where everyone deeply cares about their work, and each other, gives your company a huge competitive edge, and makes it a much more enjoyable place to be for everyone. The most effective discipline you can ever get is when staff are conscientious not through fear of their manager, but through fear of letting their colleagues down.

You spend too much time at work for it not to be fun (although it's far from always a walk in the park either – no point having TOO high expectations). It's important that everyone understands how the company functions from their first interview, and recruiting people that you feel will get on well with each other, will work equally hard, and look forward to seeing each other every day, is essential.

Never lose your sense of humour – there are times when it's the only thing that will keep you sane.

STAND UP TO BULLIES

I asked my father some years ago what was the main lesson he had learnt about people, and his immediate answer was that most people weren't as confident as they appeared to be. I have always remembered this, and believe it is absolutely true. Bullies are, almost by definition, both unhappy and lacking in confidence. In my experience clients who gave us an unnecessarily hard time (just because they felt they could) almost always backed down when I'd finally had enough and confronted them and told them I wouldn't stand for their behaviour any more, whether it was towards me or, worse, towards our staff. Valid criticism is one thing, but bullying quite another.

SILENCE IS GOLDEN

One of the best tips I've ever been given is the power of silence. Next time you're in awkward negotiations just try it. Trained negotiators – particularly buyers in large companies – will often use it as a form of intimidation, leaving lengthy gaps while you witter on about this and that just to fill the uncomfortable void. Instead, simply play them at their own game, say clearly what you want to say, and out-silence them. It works every time, and puts you back on a level footing with them.

LEARN TO SWITCH OFF

Running your own business can be a pretty intense experience and, as mentioned previously, to have the best chance of really succeeding you need to throw yourself wholeheartedly at it. It is essential, however, to be able to switch off. Everyone has different ways of doing this, and it can take some discipline, but make sure there is some balance in your life, for your own sake as well as the sake of the business. Holidays are not only good, they are essential. Make sure you take them.

EARN OR LEARN

Make sure you are always earning or learning, and preferably both. If you find yourself doing not much of either, then it's time to look for something else to do.

USE EXPERTS

If/when you come to sell your business, don't try and handle it all yourself (it'll drive you crazy, and is much more complicated than you could ever imagine) and make sure you use a company that specialises in your field and understands your business and the other players in your market. Using a company with genuine in-depth knowledge of your industry will give you a much higher chance of success.

TRUST YOUR INSTINCTS

It is too easy to think of your instincts, or 'gut feelings' as just a whim, to be casually dismissed without being taken too seriously. Instead, I believe they are incredibly important, and represent a distillation of *all* your experiences, knowledge and learning from your entire life, and are to be dismissed at your peril.

Some people like to work things out and make decisions in a very structured, almost scientific way. Personally, I have relied almost entirely on my instincts for every major decision, and any regrets I have had have generally come from when I didn't follow them.

TO AVOID SEASICKNESS, LOOK TO THE HORIZON

If the first three primary characteristics of an entrepreneur are common sense, drive, and confidence, then the fourth is tenacity. There will be endless times when things go wrong, when there seems no hope of success, when you feel like giving up, and you will have to dig very deep to keep going. During these troubled times, look to the horizon, to your main goal. It is all too easy to get bogged down navel-gazing when things are not going well, but it's rarely constructive and is a luxury you can't afford. Once you're back in the positive zone you will be in a much better position to deal with any issues that were concerning you. It also helps to physically as well as metaphorically keep your head up, whether walking down the street, or sitting at your desk; even raising the height of the monitor on your desk can help with this.

One of the interesting aspects of life in general is that everyone else's lives can seem to be much easier than your own (and their problems are of course *much* easier to solve than your own), and everyone else's business can also seem to run much more smoothly than your own. The reality is of course that everyone has to pedal pretty hard to keep going, so don't expect your business to be any different. It is also a great truism that the greater the toil, the sweeter the success.

GOOD LUCK

We all need luck. If you get some, grasp it with both hands and run with it, appreciate it, and enjoy it.